GREAT HITTERS
of the Major Leagues

Colorful profiles of eleven men who made base-
ball history because of their batting prowess: Ty
Cobb, Babe Ruth, Rogers Hornsby, Lou Gehrig,
Hank Greenberg, Joe DiMaggio, Ted Williams,
Stan Musial, Willie Mays, Mickey Mantle, and
Henry Aaron.

GREAT HITTERS of the Major Leagues

by FRANK GRAHAM, Jr.

MAJOR LEAGUE LIBRARY

PHOTOGRAPH CREDITS:

Brown Brothers: 2, 22, 27, 30, 38, 40, 56, 64; Culver Pictures: 7, 11, 16; New York Daily News: 32, 61; Pictorial Parade: 5, 108; Ken Regan–Camera Five: ii, 122, 150; Fred Roe: front endpapers, back endpapers, 94, 132, 163, 166; United Press International: 19, 28, 43, 50, 55, 62, 69, 71, 74, 76, 78, 84–85, 86, 91, 97, 101, 115, 117, 125, 134, 136, 139, 143, 146, 157, 159; Wide World: 37, 48, 88, 105, 113, 119, 127, 148, 154

Cover photo: Ken Regan

CONTENTS

ADVICE TO HITTERS

Many years ago a ballplayer named "Wee Willie" Keeler was explaining his success as a hitter. His advice was short and to the point.

"Hit 'em where they ain't," he said.

That is still the best advice anybody can give to a young hitter: to hit the ball where there aren't any fielders.

Great Hitters of the Major Leagues is about eleven ballplayers who were—or are—very good at hitting the ball where the fielders "ain't." Some, like Ty Cobb, knew how to poke the ball to all fields, just out of the reach of fielders on the other team. Others, like Rogers Hornsby and Stan Musial, could slam line drives past fielders before they had a chance to reach for them. And still others, like Babe Ruth and Mickey Mantle, swung with such great power that they hit the ball completely over the fielders' heads and into the distant stands. That is one place where you can be sure there won't be *any* fielders.

There have been other great hitters in the past besides the ones whose stories you will find in this book. Today there are players like Carl Yastrzemski and Roberto Clemente and Frank Robinson. Undoubtedly their names will be found in the books about great hitters that will be written in the future. But the eleven colorful players included here must lead every list of Great Hitters of the Major Leagues.

GREAT HITTERS
of the Major Leagues

TY COBB

The batter, wearing the uniform of the Detroit Tigers, stood at the plate waiting for the ball to be pitched. His feet were spread apart only slightly, and he gripped the bat in a curious way. Instead of holding it near the end with both hands close together on the handle, he slid his left hand up the bat so that it was four inches above his right hand. A baseball fan who had never watched Ty Cobb at bat before might have thought he was getting ready to bunt.

But then the pitch came in and Cobb swung hard, hitting the ball solidly off the right field wall. Before the right fielder could return the ball to the infield, Cobb was on second base with a double. The Detroit fans cheered their hero, but they did not relax. Though Cobb was the greatest hitter in baseball, the excitement did not die down once he had gotten his base hit. For he was also the most exciting base runner in the game. No one knew quite what he would do next.

The Tigers were playing the New York Highlanders. And this particular game took place several years before the outbreak of World War One.

Cobb took his lead off second base. The New York pitcher threw to the plate. At the crack of the bat, Cobb set out for third base. The New York first baseman fielded the ball, stepped on the base to put out the batter and then fired the ball over to third base. But Cobb, who had rounded third, kept on running for home. When the third baseman took the throw and looked for a runner to tag, Cobb already was across the plate with a run for the Tigers.

It had all happened in a flash. Or had it? Let Ty Cobb, the greatest ballplayer of his time, tell exactly what had taken place on the field.

"The play wasn't something I just made up on the spur of the moment," Cobb said afterward. "New York's first baseman was Hal Chase, one of the smartest defensive players there ever was. If you were on second base and a ball was hit to the infield and the throw was to first base, you had to watch out when you got to third. Because if you

Ty Cobb rounding third base at full speed.

rounded the bag by just this much, Chase would have the ball over there and you were dead before you could get back.

"Knowing that, I practiced on him. I'd round the bag and dive back—always just ahead of the ball. This went on for a good part of the season. What I was waiting for was the time when I had him used to it. That's exactly what happened on that day we're talking about. Chase thought I would dive back to third base as usual. But when he threw over there, I was going the other way. He had tried to trap me once too often!"

Trying to fool Ty Cobb was like playing with dynamite. He was always a step ahead of his opponents because he played the game with his mind as well as with his body. Cobb was not a "super" player to begin with. He did not have great power at bat. He did not have great running speed. And he did not have a great throwing arm. He simply tried harder, and thought faster, than any other player in baseball.

"His genius was a kind of insanity—a desire to beat you at anything in any way he could," said a man who had known Cobb well.

Ty was born in Narrows, Georgia, in 1886. His father, who was the county's superintendent of schools, wanted him to become a professional man —perhaps a doctor, or a lawyer. But Ty loved

6

A typical Cobb grip—with hands four or five inches apart.

baseball. Even as a boy, he was always dreaming up ways to beat the older boys at games. It was not easy at first. Since the others were older, they used heavier bats than he had played with. Young Ty found it hard to swing those bats around in time to hit the ball. But then he figured out that the bat would be easier to control if he held his hands four or five inches apart on the handle. He learned to bat that way and, even after he became a grown man, he never changed his batting grip.

7

By the time he was 17 years old, Ty had made up his mind that he wanted to be a big league ballplayer. His father still wanted him to be a doctor or a lawyer, and the two of them had many arguments about what the boy was going to do with his life. Finally a minister, who was a friend of the family, took Ty's father aside.

"Look, Mr. Cobb," the minister said, "Ty is just determined he's going to be a ballplayer. He's too good at playing ball *not* to be one. It's better to let him go with your approval than to have him leave home without it."

Ty's father finally agreed. Early in 1904, young Ty went off to play professional baseball. He proved to be a good judge of his own ability. By the end of the following year, he was playing center field for the Tigers in the American League. But his struggles weren't over. The great confidence and determination that helped him get to the big leagues could very easily have caused him to fail once he got there. His new teammates on the Tigers thought he tried *too* hard. He got into fights easily—with his teammates as well as with the opposing players. Soon the other Tigers refused to have anything at all to do with him off the diamond.

"I hated them as much as they hated me," Cobb once told a friend. "Later on I was grateful for what they did for me by driving me off by myself.

8

I ate alone, roomed alone and walked alone. What else could I do when I wasn't at the ball park? There weren't many movies in those days. I couldn't go to a vaudeville show every night, and I didn't want to hang around in the bowling alleys or night clubs. And I wasn't much of a reader.

"So I'd walk the streets for a couple of hours after a game. That helped to keep my legs in shape. And when I was walking or sitting in my room or lying in bed before I went to sleep I had plenty of time to think. And what else was I going to think about but baseball—how to hit pitchers, how to play the hitters in the field, and how to run the bases?"

Cobb, who had always hated to lose, now had another reason for wanting to succeed. He was determined to prove to his teammates that he was a better ballplayer than any of them. They gave him no help, of course. Usually, when a player isn't hitting well, his teammates will come to him with advice and encouragement. But if Ty Cobb had asked any of the Tigers for advice, they would very likely have given him the wrong answers!

When he went into a batting slump, Ty had to find out for himself just what he was doing wrong. "I would remind myself," he explained later on to a friend, "that I could hit any pitcher in the league. But now, for some reason, I wasn't hitting them. They didn't have any more stuff on the ball than they had the last time I saw them. My eyesight was still as good as it had ever been. I was standing at the plate the same way I always had. I held the bat the same way—but I wasn't getting hits.

"There could be only one answer. My stroke was off just a little bit. I was hitting just under the ball, or just over it. The solution was to meet the ball right in the middle. So whenever I got in a batting slump I simply tried to hit the ball right back to the pitcher. That's all I tried to do. Just flatten out my stroke, so that when the pitcher threw to me I could hit it back to him. Then, after a day or so, I was hitting the ball right on the nose, and it was going past the pitcher and I was getting hits again."

The fans always thought of Cobb as a very fast runner as well as a great hitter. Because he stole more bases than anyone else, the fans were sure he must be able to run faster than anybody else. But that wasn't quite true. Although Cobb was a fast runner, even he admitted that there were players in the league who could beat him if they ever decided to compete in a race.

"I looked faster than I was because I got the jump on an opposing player," Cobb often said. "Like in my stolen bases. When I got the jump on the pitcher, the catcher had little or no chance to throw me out, no matter how good his arm was. I could have been slower than I was and still, in many cases, he couldn't have thrown me out."

When Cobb joined the Tigers late in 1905 he batted only .240 during the rest of the season. But never again would his batting average fall below .320. In 1907 he batted .350 to lead the American League, and this was only the first of the 12 batting championships he won—nine of them in a row! In 1911 he batted .420 and stole 83 bases. The next year he came back to bat .410. In 1915 he stole 96 bases. Everyone agreed that Ty Cobb,

Safe on third . . .

"The Georgia Peach," was the greatest player in baseball.

But, though he had proved to all the world, as well as to his own teammates, that he was the very best, he did not change his way of life. And his life was *baseball*. He was always thinking up new ways to beat the other team.

Old-time fans still recall the day that the Washington Senators had to play a rookie at third base against the Tigers because their regular third baseman had been hurt. Cobb decided to see how good the rookie was. He came to bat and laid down a bunt along the third base line. The rookie rushed in and tried to grab the rolling ball, but he came up with a fistful of grass instead. By the time he was able to pick up the ball, Ty was on his way to second base. The rookie fired the ball desperately in that direction, but his throw was wild. It sailed into the outfield, and Ty raced all the way home.

Now Cobb knew where the Senators' weakness was. The next time at bat, he bunted the ball along the third base line again. The Washington rookie, eager to make up for his error, rushed in to field the ball. Once more he had trouble picking it up. Once more Cobb raced around first base and headed for second. And once more the rookie threw the ball away. As Ty scored another run for the Tigers, the Senators' manager rushed out of the dugout and took his third baseman aside.

"Look, son," he said, "the next time he bunts the ball to you, just pick it up and run back to third base with it. You might be able to head him off there!"

Success did not make Ty Cobb any easier to live with. He had to win at any price. In dugouts around the league, the other players used to joke that Ty would cut his grandmother's legs off with his spikes if she stood between him and a stolen base. It made no difference to Cobb whether he was in a championship game or an exhibition game—he played hard all the way.

In the spring of 1917 the Tigers played a series of exhibition games in the South with the New York Giants. Cobb was at the peak of his career then, but the Giants had some very tough players too. They were determined not to let Ty get away with anything. The first time he came to bat, the Giants' pitcher hit Cobb on the shoulder with the ball. As he trotted to first base, Ty snarled at the pitcher, "I'll take care of you later."

"You try any funny business with me and I'll knock your brains out!" the pitcher roared back at him.

All the Giants began to scream insults at Cobb. Then Buck Herzog, their second baseman, dared Ty to try to steal. That was all Cobb needed! On the next pitch to the plate, he broke for second. The Giant catcher, expecting him to try to steal, threw quickly to Herzog, who caught the ball in plenty of time to make the tag. And then it happened. Cobb didn't even try for the base. Instead, he slid hard into Herzog, ripping the Giant's right leg open with his spikes and knocking him down.

The incident touched off a riot on the playing field. Herzog and Cobb rolled in the dirt, clawing and punching at each other. Players, umpires and policemen swirled around them, some trying to break up the fight, others pushing each other in anger. Both players were finally thrown off the field by the umpires, and the game went on. But the incident did not end there. That night Herzog challenged Cobb to finish their fight in his hotel room. A few players from both teams were allowed in and the door was locked.

"Take off your coat and shirt," Herzog told Cobb.

Cobb stripped to his waist, and the fight began. Herzog knocked him down with the first punch he threw. Then Cobb got up and punched Herzog all over the room. The other players finally stepped in and stopped the fight to save Herzog from further punishment. Both players seemed satisfied that they had upheld their honor. Baseball was a very rough game in those days.

Cobb continued to be the best player in baseball for many more years. In 1922, at the age of 36, he batted .401. When, at the age of 42, he finally retired from professional baseball, he left behind him a string of records, many of which may never be broken. He stole a total of 892 bases and his lifetime batting average for 24 seasons in the American League was .367.

But Ty Cobb, who played only to win, accumulated more than a string of records on the baseball diamond. He played so hard that he made many enemies too.

After he retired, Cobb sometimes went out to the ball park and gave young players the sort of good advice he had never received. It was hard for those young players to believe that Cobb hadn't always been a friendly fellow.

It was necessary to have played against Ty Cobb to know that he was the toughest—as well as the greatest—player of his time.

BABE RUTH

It was the third game of the 1932 World Series between the New York Yankees and the Chicago Cubs. The Yankees had won the first two games. Now as the teams resumed the Series at Chicago's Wrigley Field, a noisy crowd filled the stands to root for the Cubs and hoot the Yankees. The two teams did not like each other. The uproar reached a peak in the third inning when Babe Ruth came to bat for the Yankees.

Ruth, the greatest slugger of all time, had been taunting the Cubs from the beginning of the Series. Now, as he stepped up to bat against the Cubs' veteran pitcher, Charlie Root, the crowd was getting back at him. So were the Cubs, who shrieked insults at Ruth from their dugout. Ruth paid no attention, but dug in at the plate.

The Cubs' pitcher threw a fast ball over the plate and Ruth watched it go by. Without waiting for the umpire to rule on it, the Babe simply held up one finger, signaling that it was a strike. On the next pitch he did the same thing, watching the ball go by, and then holding up two fingers to signal that it was strike two. The crowd was roaring at him in anger. Was the great Babe just pulling a fancy stunt? Ruth turned and grinned at the Cubs' dugout, then stepped back into the batter's box.

Root, the Cubs' pitcher, got ready to throw again. At that moment, the Babe lifted his right arm and pointed in the direction of the distant right-field wall. Then the pitch came in. Swinging, the Babe hit a tremendous drive deep and high to right field. As the crowd came to its feet in disbelief, the ball sailed over the wall at the spot to which the Babe had pointed only a moment before.

It was the most cocksure gesture in the history of baseball. Had the Babe actually been telling the fans that he would hit *that* pitch over the wall at *that* point, the newspapermen asked him after the game?

"It was the greatest thing I ever saw," one of the reporters told him. "But if you'd missed that ball, you sure would have looked like a sucker."

The Babe slugs a homer in the 1932 World Series.

"By gosh, that's right," Ruth answered. "I never thought of that!"

It would never have occurred to the Babe that he might fail, because his entire career was one triumphal experience. If any other player had attempted such a stunt in an important game, he would have been called a braggart or a fool. But the Babe was different. He was the most colorful player in the history of baseball. Whatever he did, on or off the field, was all right with the fans. When he hit a home run, it was a gigantic one. When he had a belly ache, it was also gigantic.

The Babe had not always been on top of the world. In fact, during his boyhood days no one would have given a nickel for his chances of making a success of himself. Born George Herman Ruth, in 1895, he was the son of a saloon keeper in a poor neighborhood in Baltimore. There were seven other children in the family, but the Babe was the most difficult to control. Finally his parents sent him to St. Mary's Industrial Home for Boys. There, fed and clothed by the Roman Catholic brothers who ran the school, George Herman Ruth grew into an awkward teen-ager. One of the men who took an interest in the boy was Brother Gilbert. He has since told of the first time he ever saw Ruth.

"I was at St. Mary's one day, and I had seen this boy who, as far as I was concerned, was just a big kid in blue overalls. He was catching for one of the teams in a league they had at St. Mary's, and if you ever wanted to see a bone out of joint or one of nature's misfits, you should have seen him. He was a left-handed catcher, squatting behind home plate. All he had on was a mask and a glove, which he wore on his left hand. When he had to make a throw to second base he would take off the glove and tuck it under his right arm before he made the throw. And how he could throw! The ball was three feet off the ground going through the pitcher's box and three feet off the ground when it got to second base."

Brother Gilbert talked to baseball men in Baltimore about this youngster. He told them that anyone who could throw the ball so hard would make an outstanding pitcher. Soon the Babe was signed to a contract. He wanted so much to play ball that he was amazed when he learned that the local team would *pay* him for it. Within a year he was pitching in the big leagues for the Boston Red Sox.

Fans are inclined to think of Babe Ruth simply as a great slugger. Most of them do not remember that he was probably the greatest all-around player the game has known. When he was with the Red Sox, he was the best left-handed pitcher in the American League. In 1915 he won 18 games, then came back to lead the Red Sox to the pennant in 1916 by winning 23 games. In the World Series, they beat the Dodgers, 4–1. He won 23 games again in 1917, then helped the Red Sox to win the pennant and the World Series in 1918. One of his victories in that World Series was a shutout.

Meanwhile, the Red Sox were discovering that Ruth was even more of a help to them as a batter. Home runs were not very common in those days. It was rare for a pitcher to hit any home runs at all. But the Babe had tremendous power. Throughout the league, the other players were talking about how far this young left-handed slugger could hit the ball. And he made an imposing

With the Red Sox, Babe Ruth earned a reputation as the best left-handed pitcher in the American League.

figure at the plate—a big moon-faced fellow, with a flat nose and a barrel-like body. Most curious of all, that huge body was set on slender legs which looked as if they could not support a man half his size.

Soon the Red Sox began to use Ruth in the outfield on days when he wasn't pitching. Then, in 1920, they startled the baseball world by selling the Babe to the Yankees. The Red Sox needed the money. The Yankees immediately saw that Ruth could become the most exciting player in baseball. They told him to forget about pitching. From now on he would be an outfielder, and he would take his place in the line-up every day.

In the course of that single season Babe Ruth changed the whole style of the game. Until then, baseball had been dominated by the players who collected a lot of singles and doubles, beat out bunts and stole bases. Ty Cobb, of course, was the expert at that. But the Babe made the home run the most important weapon in baseball. He hit 54 homers during the season. This total was almost twice that of the old big league record of 29 home runs, which the Babe himself had set during the previous year at Boston.

Suddenly fans were flocking into the ball parks as they never had before. The Yankees drew thousands of people wherever they played, and most of them came because of Babe Ruth. "This new fan didn't know where first base was," a baseball reporter once wrote, "but he had heard of Babe Ruth and wanted to see him hit a home run. When the Babe hit one, the fan went back the next day to see him hit another. Pretty soon he was a regular, and knew not only where first base was but second base as well."

Babe Ruth had now taken the place of Ty Cobb as the most exciting player in baseball.

No two men could have been farther apart in the way they looked at baseball and at life. All Cobb thought about was the game. But Ruth, when the game was over, thought only about having a good time. He did not sit around in his room at night, figuring out ways to beat the other fellow. For a while he roomed with a player named Ping Bodie, but Ping seldom saw him. One day someone asked Ping whom he roomed with.

"I room with a suitcase," Ping said.

Ball clubs did not travel by plane in those days. On long trips they took the train. When the Yankees had short trips to make to other cities in the East, such as Boston and Philadelphia, their manager allowed them to go by automobile. Ruth, of course, had the biggest and the fastest car, and the other players liked to travel with him because he was fun to be with.

On one of these trips, the Babe had several of his teammates in the car with him, as well as Charlie O'Leary, a coach. He was speeding along, singing at the top of his voice and laughing with the others, when suddenly the car went out of control. It skidded into a curve and turned over. By a miracle, no one in the car seemed to be hurt. But then Babe noticed that O'Leary had been thrown out and was lying motionless in the road.

The Babe rushed over to where the coach lay like a dead man. "Oh, God! Bring him back! Don't let him die! Take me instead!" the Babe moaned.

O'Leary still lay there, motionless.

"Speak to me, Charlie! Speak to me!" the Babe begged.

At that moment O'Leary sat up and looked around.

"Hey," he hollered, "where the heck is my new straw hat?"

The Babe pushed him on his back again and walked away.

But no matter how much fun the Babe had had the night before, or how late he had stayed up, he was always ready to play ball the next day. Until he joined them, the Yankees had been a losing team. Now suddenly they were a success, and Ruth was their star. In 1923 they opened their new ball park—Yankee Stadium. It was the finest baseball stadium in the world. The newspapers called it "The House That Ruth Built," because the crowds attracted by the Babe had provided the money to pay for it. On the day that the stadium opened, more than 60,000 fans crowded in to see this beautiful new ball park—and to watch Babe Ruth. The Babe did not disappoint them. He hit a home run with two men on and the Yankees won the game, 4–1.

The Yankees were winning pennants now, too. Whenever they needed a big hit, they looked to the Babe. He was always there to help out in any situation. One afternoon the Yankees were playing the White Sox in Chicago. The game went into extra innings, tied 1–1. The Yankee officials had made reservations for the team to board a train to New York right after the game. Now, as inning after inning went by, they began to worry that they would miss the train.

In the fifteenth inning, Ruth noticed that one of the Yankee officials was acting fidgety.

"What's worrying you?" he asked as he grabbed a bat and prepared to go to the plate. "Are you sick?"

"You bet I am," the official answered. "If you bums don't finish this game in a hurry, we're all going to miss the train."

"Take it easy," Babe said. "I'll get us out of here."

The Babe went up to bat and hit the first pitch out of the park. As he came back to the dugout, he looked over at the official and grinned.

"Okay," he said. "See you in the taxicab."

There were times when the Babe had his troubles. He was the biggest eater, as well as the greatest home-run hitter, in baseball. He ate enormous quantities of hot dogs, and drank enormous quantities of soda pop. Naturally, he often

Safe at third during the World Series of 1923.

had stomach aches. As a rule, they did not stop
him from playing. But in 1925, as he was standing on a platform at a railroad station, he doubled
over in pain and had to be rushed to the hospital.
Too many hot dogs and soft drinks for breakfast,
the doctors said. For a while he was in very bad
shape. Some newspapers even reported that he
was dying. The whole country became concerned
about the condition of this famous man, and one
reporter even wrote that the Babe had developed
"the world's most important stomach ache."

But soon the Babe was back on the playing
field, leading the Yankees to championships.

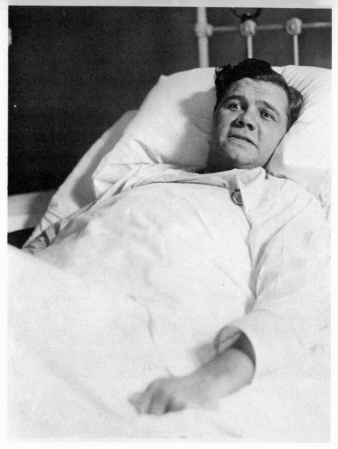

Hospitalized, the Babe enjoyed the "world's most important stomach ache."

Wherever he went, crowds lined up to see him. If people in a small town learned that the Babe was on a train which would stop there during the night, they would all come down to the railroad station to get a look at him. And the Babe never failed them. Even if he had been sound asleep, he would get himself up, put on his bathrobe and walk out onto the platform to wave at the crowds.

He was a favorite wherever he went. One day

the Yankees played an exhibition game at Sing Sing Prison. The Babe came to bat and hit a home run far over the prison wall.

"Oh, boy, I'd like to be riding that one," a convict yelled.

The Babe loved it. When one of the prisoners, who was acting as umpire, called one of the Yankees out on a close play, Ruth ran over to him and yelled, "Robber!"

The prisoners enjoyed it as much as the Babe did.

Ruth was always genuinely fond of children. Whenever he heard that a child was ill, he tried to do something about it. Many times, as soon as a game was over, the Babe would hurry to get dressed and rush to a hospital to see some child who was ill.

"I'll hit a home run for you tomorrow, kid," he would say.

And, as often as not, he kept his promise.

The Babe occasionally had arguments with his teammates, of course. He was a great player, and he expected other players to come through in the clutch just as he did. He even criticized the Yankees' manager. One year, however, the manager had enough of Babe and the way he appeared late at the ball park every day. He fined him $5,000. That was a record too!

But for the most part his teammates liked and

Ruth hits his sixtieth home run for the 1927 season.

admired the Babe just as the fans did. It didn't even bother them that he had a hard time remembering their names. He knew the names of a few of the men he had played with for a long time, but he just couldn't remember the others. So he made up names for them. He called one Yankee pitcher "Rubber Belly," and another "Chicken Neck." He knew an infielder as "Flop Ears," and another pitcher as "Duck Eye." Nobody seemed to mind his new name, as long as it came from the Babe.

Ruth hit 60 home runs in 1927, and ended his career with a total of 714. It is not likely that any player ever will approach that record. Yet, though most home run hitters do not hit for a high average, the Babe also finished his career with a lifetime batting average of .342.

"I could have hit .600 every year if I'd wanted to," he once told a friend. "The way they used to play for me, with the infielders back on the edge of the grass and the outfielders out by the fences and everybody swung around to the right, I could have rolled a bunt anywhere in the infield or popped the ball into short left field and walked to first base."

"Why didn't you?" his friend asked.

"Because," the Babe said, "the people paid to see me hit home runs." And the Babe always gave the people their money's worth.

ROGERS HORNSBY

Some years ago, at the spring training camp of the old St. Louis Browns, many of the fans and reporters were raving about the fielding skill of a rookie infielder. The manager of the Browns overheard their comments and snorted in disgust.

"You can have the fancy fielders," he said. "Just find me the hitters. The fielders you can shake out of the trees by the dozen."

The manager of the Browns was Rogers Hornsby, retired by then as a player but remembered by the fans as the greatest right-handed hitter they had ever seen. Soon the little group of fans had forgotten the fancy fielder and were watching the batting cage instead. There, another rookie was taking batting practice. Hornsby began to give the boy some advice, and it was the sort of lesson that anyone interested in batting could profit from.

"You know where your head was on that pitch, son?" Hornsby said, as he peered through the wire netting of the cage. "It was clear out in left field. How do you expect to hit the ball if you don't look at it?"

Turning to his listeners again, Hornsby went on to talk some more about hitting.

"You've got to teach young players to follow the ball all the way to the bat," he said. "Follow it with their eyes until they've swung at it. They swing where they *think* the ball is. Trouble is that the ball so often breaks sharply at the last second, and when they turn their head they're swinging where the ball used to be. That's what makes them look so silly on some pitches. A hitter seldom will go after a bad pitch if he sees it all the way from the pitcher's hand until it reaches the plate."

Few men have ever known as much about the art of hitting a baseball as Rogers Hornsby. When he spoke about batting, fans, writers—and even other ballplayers—listened. Yet, curiously enough, it was not on the basis of his hitting that Hornsby reached the major leagues.

Rogers Hornsby was born on a ranch outside

Winters, Texas, in 1896. After his father died, the family moved to Fort Worth, where young Rogers served as the batboy for a local team which was sponsored by a meat-packing firm. During practice the older players allowed him to join in, and he picked up some tips about fielding and hitting. When he was 18 years old, he became a minor league player.

Hornsby was a good fielder with strong, sure hands, and he made a place for himself as a shortstop on Texas teams. Yet he batted only .232 in his first season, and .277 the next. Unfortunately he was a tall, skinny fellow who lacked the strength to hold and swing the bat properly. Instead, he gripped it several inches from the end. When he swung at the ball, he looked like a boy trying to poke a turtle off a log with a stick.

A scout for the St. Louis Cardinals saw Hornsby play. "I liked him," the scout said later. "He didn't hit very much, but he could field his position and he handled himself like a ballplayer."

The Cardinals needed players very badly. They paid the minor league team $700 for Hornsby's contract, and Rogers went to St. Louis late in the 1915 season. It wasn't easy for him at first. The pitchers made him look bad. In one game he faced Grover Cleveland Alexander of the Philadelphia Phillies, who was the finest pitcher in the National League. Alexander struck out

Hornsby the first two times the rookie came to bat. Late in the game, when the Phillies had a comfortable lead, their catcher went out to the mound.

"Here's that Hornsby kid again," he told Alexander. "Why don't you give him a break and let him hit the ball? It'll make him feel good."

An easy-going man, Alexander agreed. He tossed a soft pitch to Hornsby, and the rookie pounded it up against the left-field wall for a double.

Long afterward, Alexander recalled that moment. "You know," he said, "I didn't get that Hornsby out again for 15 years!"

No one ever had to give Hornsby another break. With a little experience he became an established big league player. The Cardinals eventually moved him to second base, and that became his position for the rest of his long career. No one was better than Hornsby at scooping up grounders or pivoting on the double play. His only weakness was the way he drifted back under pop flies. He never mastered that art, and the fans used to hold their breath when he started to circle around under a high pop fly. They were by no means certain that he would catch it.

But once his slender frame filled out, Hornsby had no weaknesses as a hitter. He held the bat down near the end of the handle and stood far

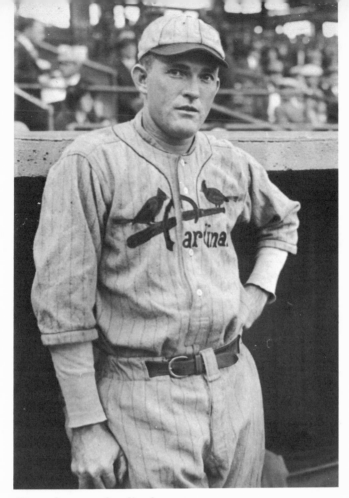

Hornsby as a Cardinal.

away from the plate, deep in the batter's box. When the pitcher delivered the ball, Hornsby stepped into the pitch, bringing his bat around in a crisp, level swing. He did not hit the long, high home runs that Ruth drove out of the ball park, but he hit savage line drives. No one liked to get in the way of a ball hit by Rogers Hornsby.

No one was better than Hornsby at scooping up grounders.

Old-timers still tell the story about the day the Dodgers sent in a rookie to pitch to Hornsby. The rookie pitcher called Jack Fournier, the veteran first baseman, over to the mound.

"How should I pitch to Hornsby?" the rookie asked.

"Throw him a fast ball on the inside corner," Fournier told him.

The rookie did as he was told. Hornsby smashed the inside pitch down the left-field line. The ball almost tore off the third baseman's pant leg as it shot past him. Hornsby wound up on second base with a double. The rookie pitcher walked over to Fournier.

"I thought you said he couldn't hit a pitch on the inside corner!" the rookie exclaimed.

"I didn't say that," Fournier said. "I got a wife and a family to think about and I didn't want that fellow hitting any outside pitches my way."

In 1921 Hornsby began the most spectacular stretch of successful hitting in baseball history. In that year he batted .397. His batting averages for the next four seasons were .401, .384, .424 and .403. His .424 average in 1924 was the highest ever made in the big leagues.

In the 1923 World Series, the New York Giants were pitted against the Yankees and Babe Ruth. The Giant manager, John McGraw, was asked if he was afraid of the Babe. McGraw shook his head.

"Listen," he said, "for years we've been pitching to a better hitter than Ruth in our own league— Rogers Hornsby."

One of the secrets of Hornsby's success as a hitter was his marvelously keen eyes. If he thought that the pitch was going to be only an inch off the corner of the plate, he would not swing at it. "Hornsby got more *fourth* strikes than any other hitter in baseball," one of his teammates said of him. What the player meant

Rogers held the bat down near the end of the handle.

was that if Hornsby let the pitch go by, the umpire simply figured that it *must* have been wide of the plate and so did not call it a strike.

Despite his great skill with a bat, Hornsby never received the public acclaim that came to Cobb and Ruth. He did not run the bases and knock down opposing players the way Cobb did. Nor did he hit mighty home runs like the Babe. Off the field, Hornsby was very much like Cobb. He did not drink or smoke, and kept very much to himself. He would not even go to the movies because he believed they might hurt his eyes.

"Baseball is my life," Hornsby said. "It's the only thing I know and can talk about. Some of the other fellows like to play golf in their spare time but I'm not old enough for a sport like that. I'm used to having other guys chase the balls I hit. I'll be damned if I'm going to run after a little white ball myself!"

In 1926, while he was still the best hitter in the league, he was appointed the manager of the Cardinals. Up to that time no St. Louis team had ever won a pennant, and it seemed unlikely that they would win one that year. But the Cardinals caught fire under Hornsby. Perhaps they became inspired by their manager's complete devotion to the game. In any case, they won their first pennant and entered the World Series against Babe Ruth and the mighty Yankees.

Just as the Series was beginning, Hornsby's mother died in Texas. Everyone expected that he would go home for her funeral, but Hornsby announced that he would stay with his team until after the World Series.

"My mother knew she was dying," Hornsby explained. "She knew also that this World Series meant a lot to me. So she made me promise that I wouldn't come home until it was over."

This strange, intense man then turned his attention to the job of beating the Yankees. Only when the last out had been made, and his Cardinals were the baseball champions of the world, did Hornsby get on a train and go back to Texas to bury his mother.

Hornsby was a hero to the fans for bringing the championship to St. Louis at last. But he was not a hero to the men he worked for, or the players who worked under him. A lonely and self-centered man, he said exactly what he thought. It never occurred to him to keep his mouth shut and spare the other fellow some discomfort. In fact, he never spared *himself* any discomfort. When Sam Breadon, the owner of the Cardinals, scheduled an exhibition game on an off day while the tired Cardinals were struggling to win the pennant, Hornsby didn't hesitate to express his feelings.

"Breadon knew we were all tired, but he

couldn't resist picking up a few more dollars," Hornsby told the press. "That man is a cheap-skate!"

Though he had never paid much attention to his teammates before, Hornsby became hard on them once he was named their manager. When they complained about how tough he was, he simply shrugged.

"I'm running a ball club, not a popularity contest," he said.

As a manager, Hornsby worked his men hard.

Because the fans didn't know the whole story, they were shocked after the World Series when the Cardinals announced that they had traded Hornsby to the Giants. Rogers was not only the most feared hitter in the league, but also the manager who had led the Cardinals to their first championship.

Although Hornsby was no longer a manager, the Giants expected him to lead them to a pennant with his bat. He had a fine year in 1927, batting .361, but the Giants did not think it was good enough. In reality, it was the Giants themselves who were not good enough, as Hornsby realized. Most players would have kept the knowledge to themselves. Hornsby was different. One evening he was having dinner with the Giants' shortstop, Eddie Farrell. A newspaperman stopped at the table and asked Hornsby if he thought the Giants were going to win the pennant.

Hornsby shook his head. "Not with Farrell playing shortstop," he said.

As a result, Hornsby was not any more popular with his teammates than he had been in St. Louis. When the Giants lost the pennant that season, they traded Hornsby to the Boston Braves. The Braves had a poor team in 1928, with no chance to win the pennant. And, when Hornsby himself got off to a poor start, many people in New York felt the Giants had done well to get rid of him.

44

Their belief was strengthened by the fact that Andy Cohen, who had replaced Hornsby at second base for the Giants, got off to a good start. One of the newspapers even began to print a box on the sports page, comparing the records of the two players.

"They're putting that kid Cohen on the spot," Hornsby said scornfully. "Once I get going, I'll outhit him by one hundred points."

Hornsby soon began to hit as he knew he would. By the end of the season he had outhit Cohen by 107 points. Cohen batted .274, and Hornsby .381. The Braves did not win the pennant, but neither did the Giants. After the season one of the newspapermen wrote the following verse:

> *Old Rogers Hornsby was a bum,*
> *So everybody reckoned.*
> *But Rogers led the league at bat,*
> *The Giants finished second!*

The next season, Hornsby was on the move again. The Braves traded him to the Cubs. He remained a dangerous hitter for several seasons, but he was near the end of his career. When he retired as a player he became a manager, but his sharp tongue kept him in trouble. Owners of big league teams like to think they have good players. But when they asked Hornsby for an opinion, he always told them the truth.

"Do you see any improvement in our team?" one of the owners asked Hornsby.

"They're *still* a bunch of humpty-dumpties," Hornsby said.

Despite his hard-boiled manner and his direct way of speaking, many fans and writers liked to listen to him because of his great knowledge of the game. He had a colorful way of speaking, too. Once he mentioned the fingers of catchers who had been in baseball for a long time. Those fingers, he said, were usually twisted and knotted because of all the foul tips which had smashed into them.

"Shaking hands with an old catcher," he said, "is like sticking your hand into a bag of peanuts."

But it was hitting he liked to talk about most. He could always help a young player who would listen to him.

"I don't think you should try to change a boy's stance at the plate," he said. "At least not until he proves that he can't hit that way. The main thing is to teach him to swing at balls in the strike zone—between his shoulders and his knees and around the plate. The trouble is that when you tell a boy something and it doesn't work wonders right away, he loses confidence and goes back to doing it the old way. That's the worst thing he can do because he has been hitting about .270 at

46

most. So what have they got to lose by stringing along for a while with some good advice?"

Rogers Hornsby may not have known very much about getting along with other people. But he knew almost everything there was to know about hitting a baseball.

LOU GEHRIG

In 1923, Paul Krichell, who was a scout for the
Yankees, placed a telephone call to his boss at
the Yankees' office.

"I think I saw another Babe Ruth today,"
Krichell said.

The other man was silent for a moment, then
laughed.

"All right," Krichell said. "Laugh if you want
to. But I saw a kid playing for Columbia University today who looks like another Babe Ruth."

Krichell's boss had laughed because the Babe
was at the very peak of his career then. It didn't
seem possible that there could be a young man
anywhere in the world who could hit a baseball
even remotely like him. But Krichell had good

Lou Gehrig played football at the High School of Commerce in New York City.

reason to get excited. He was talking about a husky athlete named Lou Gehrig, who played for Columbia. Krichell, a smart baseball man, had seen Gehrig hit home runs to such distant points that only the Babe himself could have matched them.

Krichell was not the first observer to link this young man's name with Babe Ruth. Gehrig had been born in 1903 in the heart of New York City, where he grew up on the sidewalks and playgrounds of the city. Later he played football and baseball at the High School of Commerce. While Lou was there, the school had the best baseball team in the city. In 1920, having won the city championship, the team was invited to play Chicago's champions, Lane Technical High School, in an inter-city game.

The game was played at Wrigley Field, home of the Chicago Cubs. The score was tied in the ninth inning when Gehrig came to bat with the bases filled. Then, to the astonishment of the crowd, this high school boy hit one of the longest home runs ever seen at Wrigley Field—a towering smash that sailed over the distant right-field wall and out of sight. The next day, newspapers all over the country carried stories about the feat of this "High School Babe Ruth."

Baseball scouts were very much interested in Gehrig. But Lou's mother and father, who had always been poor, were eager to have their only son receive a good college education. Because of his skill on the baseball field, college coaches were interested in him too. After his graduation from high school, Lou accepted a scholarship at Columbia University.

It seemed an ideal choice, for he could still be near his parents. He thought his mother was the best cook in the world. Mrs. Gehrig, like her husband, had come to the United States from

Germany, and she prepared many old-fashioned German dishes. Lou's favorite was pickled eels. Later, when people asked him where he got his tremendous power, Lou would grin and say:

"Pickled eels!"

At Columbia, he proved to be a truly outstanding player. Like the Babe, he was a left-handed pitcher. And, like the Babe, he took his place in the outfield or at first base between turns on the pitcher's mound. When Krichell saw him in 1923, the scout decided that the Yankees must have him. At the end of the school year, Gehrig put away his books and went down to join his new team at Yankee Stadium.

He was not an immediate success, however. Although he had established himself as a powerful hitter, he was still an awkward boy who had trouble as soon as the other team came to bat. The Yankees thought he lacked the "stuff" to be a great pitcher and besides, they wanted his bat in the line-up every day. Lou wasn't a big league outfielder either. When the other players saw how he staggered around under high flies, they were afraid he might get hit on the head by a ball.

The Yankees finally decided that first base seemed to be the position Lou was best suited for, and they sent him to the minor leagues to learn how to play the position. By 1925 he was back at the stadium, eager for a chance to break into the regular line-up. It was a good time for a young player to arrive there. The Yankees, successful ever since they had bought Babe Ruth from the Red Sox, were suddenly having a bad season. Some of the older players were wearing out. The Babe himself had been put out of action by trying to stuff down too many hot dogs and sodas. While he moaned about his enormous stomach ache, the Yankee owners moaned about the quality of their ball club.

On June first, Gehrig was sent up to bat as a pinch-hitter late in the game. And the next day, when the Yankees' regular first baseman did not feel well, Gehrig was told to take his place. The rest is baseball history! The young slugger from the sidewalks of New York would not miss another game with the Yankees for almost 14 years.

The Yankees finished in seventh place that year. But in 1926 Gehrig established himself as a real major league star. Lou, the Babe and outfielder Bob Meusel teamed up to become the most fearsome group of sluggers the game had ever seen. The Yankees began to accumulate another string of pennants, powered by what the sports writers called "Murderers' Row."

"Those fellows not only beat you but they tear your heart out," an opposing player said of the Yankees. "I wish the season was over."

Facing the Yankees one afternoon, a pitcher on

53

the Cleveland Indians decided that he would try to cut down the power of Murderers' Row by pitching every ball outside to them. But the left-handed Ruth reached out and slashed a pitch off the shoulder of the Indians' third baseman, Rube Lutzke. Gehrig, also a left-handed batter, tagged a pitch that hit Lutzke on the shin and knocked him down. The pitcher, feeling that he was not having much success, threw the ball inside to the right-handed Meusel. Meusel hit a savage line drive that hit Lutzke in the stomach and knocked him down again. His teammates rushed over to try to help their unfortunate teammate to his feet.

"Are you hurt, Rube?" one of the players asked.

"Am I hurt?" Rube hollered. "Why, a guy would have been safer in the World War!"

Pitchers around the league did not know what to do about the Yankees. A few years earlier, if Ruth had come to bat with men on bases, they would have walked him. Now, if they walked Ruth, they saw Gehrig step menacingly into the batter's box. In 1927, Ruth hit 60 home runs—an all-time record for a 154-game season. But Gehrig was not far behind. That year he hit 47 homers, led the league in runs batted in (175) and posted a batting average of .373. He was voted the Most Valuable Player in the American League.

Yet Lou always stood in the shadow of Babe Ruth. It was the Babe who gathered the headlines

The new Yankee slugger hits a homer.

The Babe and Lou.

and drew the cheers of the crowd. Not that Lou
was unpopular with the fans or the other players.
Everybody who knew the soft-spoken Gehrig liked
him. The Babe was simply a more colorful charac-
ter who did everything in such a grand manner
that he was always in the spotlight. Gehrig
pounded enemy pitchers just as thoroughly, but
the Babe got the headlines.

One of the most obvious differences between

the two players was their temperaments. If the Babe had a bad day at bat, he forgot it as soon as the game was over and went out to have a good time. Lou worried when he was not hitting well. Once, when he was in a bad slump, Lou went to one of the older players.

"What am I doing wrong?" he asked.

"I don't know," the older player said.

When Gehrig shook his head sadly and walked away, the older player said to a friend of his:

"I think I know what he's doing wrong but I'm not going to tell him. He's asking everybody on the ball club what's wrong with him. And everybody is telling him something different. If I told him, it would only add to the confusion. He won't come out of the slump until he gets desperate enough to quit worrying."

Lou came out of his slump, of course, because he was a great hitter. Soon, he and the Babe were tormenting enemy pitchers again.

In a 1931 game, Gehrig had a chance to grab a few headlines for himself. Coming to bat with infielder Lyn Lary on first base, Lou smashed the ball over the fence and began to trot around the bases. But Lary thought the ball had been caught. Instead of trotting around too, he went to the dugout to get his glove and take his position in the field. Gehrig did not notice what had happened. He kept going until he had completed his tour of the bases. At this point the umpires ruled that Gehrig was out for having passed Lary on the base paths. He had lost a home run!

The other players were furious with Lary. They felt he had done a stupid thing. But Gehrig, as usual, did not criticize anybody but himself.

"Lary's no more to blame than I am," he said. "If I had kept my head up, I would have seen what happened and waited for him to come back and touch the plate before I scored."

The incident did not seem very important at the time. But when the season was over, Ruth and Gehrig were tied for the big league lead in home runs with 46 apiece. If that other homer had counted, Gehrig would have had the championship all to himself.

By 1934 the Babe was nearing the end of his career. Gehrig tore the league apart that year. He led the American League in home runs, runs batted in and batting. Then in 1936 he received the Most Valuable Player Award. With Ruth's retirement, it seemed that Lou now would have the headlines to himself.

But just after Ruth retired, another glamorous player arrived in New York. His name was Joe DiMaggio. Once more, Gehrig seemed destined to play second fiddle to a more spectacular star. Lou, being the kind of man he was, did not let this worry him. As long as he kept hitting the ball solidly, he was happy.

But now Gehrig was getting his name in the papers for a very special reason. Someone had discovered that he had not missed a game since that day in 1925 when he had gone up to pinch-hit during the late innings. He had played in more than 1500 consecutive games, and there was no end in sight. No other player had ever chalked up such a record. The papers began to call Gehrig "The Iron Man of Baseball."

He was an iron man—no doubt about it. There was no softness in him. Once, coming back to the dugout after taking batting practice, he pushed aside the cushion on the Yankees' bench before sitting down.

"Well, I'm a son of a gun," the Yankee manager said. "We go to the trouble of putting a cushion on the bench so you players will be comfortable and then you lift it up and sit on the hard wood. What's the matter with you, anyway?"

"Nothing." Gehrig grinned. "Only I get tired of sitting on cushions. Cushions in my car. Cushions on the chairs at home. Everywhere I go there are cushions!"

This was the sort of hardness that allowed Gehrig to go on playing day after day despite injuries or illness that would have put softer men out of the line-up. Gehrig suffered injuries just like other players. He was hit in the head by a high inside pitch. He broke his thumb. But he shook off the injuries and, when it was time to start the next game, Lou was on first base as usual. There were pains in his back too. Lou told everybody it was lumbago. The pains could not keep him out of the line-up either.

But in 1938, something began to happen to the iron man. One day he would hit the ball just like the feared slugger of old. But the next day he would hit the ball "right on the nose," as the ballplayers say, and it would not go anywhere. The fans began to poke fun at Gehrig. During the off season he had played the part of a cowboy in a movie called "Rawhide."

"Hey, Rawhide!" they would yell at him. "Throw that bat away and go get your gun. You'll do better that way."

Nobody took Lou's slump seriously. He had always worked his way out of slumps before. But this time was different. The great power that had made him "another Babe Ruth" seemed to have drained out of him. Perhaps a good rest after the season would help.

But when the 1939 season began, Lou was even worse. Now he could hardly stoop over to pick up a ground ball. One day early in the season Gehrig went to Joe McCarthy, the Yankee manager, and said he was taking himself out of the game.

The Iron Man of Baseball.

Gehrig sits on the bench after asking Manager Joe McCarthy (right) to take him out of the line-up.

"Why?" McCarthy asked.

"For the good of the team," Gehrig said. "I know that I can't play ball any more."

And so after 2,130 consecutive games, Gehrig left the Yankee line-up. His teammates and the fans believed that he would return after a rest, but they were wrong. Gehrig was a sick man. He did not realize how sick he was until he went to the hospital. There the doctors told him what was the matter. He had a rare disease called amyotrophic lateral sclerosis for which there was no cure. Within two years he would be dead.

Later that season almost 80,000 fans crowded into Yankee Stadium for "Lou Gehrig Appreciation Day." This was the day on which the fans, his friends and his teammates told Gehrig how much they loved him. They showered him with presents and made speeches in which they told the world how much Gehrig had meant to them as a ballplayer and as a human being. Lou was a shy man who did not like to make speeches. And, by this time, he was so weak that he could barely walk. But he shuffled up to the microphone which stood at home plate and thanked the fans for their thoughtfulness.

"I may have been given a bad break," he told them in a halting voice, "but I have an awful lot to live for. With all this, I consider myself the luckiest man on the face of the earth."

HANK GREENBERG

"Many a day when I was a rookie," Hank Greenberg once said, "I went to the ball park hoping
it would rain. I was fearful of going out there to
play. Many a time while I was waiting to hit I
watched the hitter up there with a couple of men
on bases and two out—and I hoped he would
strike out so I wouldn't have to go up there and
hit too."

Although it's hard to believe that a great hitter
like Hank Greenberg could ever have been afraid
to go to bat, we have his own word that that was
just how he felt when he first entered the big
leagues.

"All ballplayers—or at least players with brains
and imagination—are fearful when they are new

to the big leagues," Greenberg said. "Some of them never get over it. I could tell you stories of veteran ballplayers who dread going to bat in a pinch although they are good hitters. I hear players come into the clubhouse before a game and say, 'I hope it rains today.' "

Greenberg had brains and imagination. Perhaps in the beginning those qualities made it tougher for him to succeed in the big leagues. Hank was able to imagine what it would be like to fail, and that made him nervous when he had to go to bat in a close ball game. But, in the end, the same brains and imagination helped him to overcome his fears. He went on to become one of baseball's greatest hitters.

During his early years, Greenberg's story was much the same as that of Lou Gehrig. Hank was born in New York City in 1911. In fact, he was born almost within sight of Yankee Stadium. As Hank grew up (and he grew very large indeed) he made the Yankees his heroes. He hoped someday to play in the major leagues and hit mighty home runs like Ruth and Gehrig.

Actually, Greenberg came very close to putting on a New York uniform. While he was playing baseball in high school, he began to make a name for himself. Paul Krichell, the same Yankee scout who signed Gehrig, went to watch Greenberg play. He saw a giant of a boy, standing six feet four inches tall, who hit with tremendous power. In the field, Greenberg was clumsy, often tripping over his own feet as he tried to catch the ball. But Krichell remembered how clumsy Gehrig had been as a young fellow, and he decided to try to sign Greenberg for the Yankees.

But at that time Gehrig was still young and strong and rapidly becoming the best first baseman in baseball. Greenberg happened to be a first baseman too. And his intelligence made him realize that if he signed with the Yankees he would have to sit on the bench, waiting for Gehrig to grow old. When the Detroit Tigers made Hank an offer, he decided that he had better accept it.

After spending several years in the minor leagues, Greenberg joined the Tigers in 1933. Because of his great size, everybody in Detroit expected him to be a dangerous hitter right from the start. But Hank still needed experience. His fielding had not improved very much since the days when he was tripping over his own feet on a high school diamond. But instead of simply hoping that he would become a better first baseman after a few years with the Tigers, he practiced for long hours before a game. He even paid young players to hit ground balls to him. Slowly he began to improve.

Greenberg's hitting was another matter. He had terrific power at the plate, and he was always dangerous. Yet some of the smarter pitchers in the league could fool young Hank. He struck out more often than he thought he should. What made matters worse was that he worried about his ability to hit safely with men on base. He dreaded the hoots of the crowd if he failed.

But Hank was playing with a good team. If he failed in the clutch, another player could come up with the important hit. While the better pitchers gave him a hard time, Hank collected enough home runs against lesser pitchers to stay in the Tigers' line-up.

The Tigers won the pennant in 1934, and Hank found himself in the World Series, playing against the St. Louis Cardinals. He did all right, too, except when the great Dizzy Dean was pitching for the Cardinals. Then he had trouble, because Dizzy did not give him any good pitches to hit. Hank, in fact, looked so bad to Dizzy that the great pitcher thought he could do anything he wanted with him. In the final game of the Series, when the Cardinals had a big lead, Dean called his manager to the pitcher's mound.

"Hey," Dizzy asked, "is there anything this big guy *can* hit?"

"Sure," the Cardinals' manager said. "He murders a high fast ball."

Dizzy stepped back on the mound and threw Greenberg a high fast ball. Hank hammered it

Greenberg slides safely into home plate during the 1934 World Series.

into left field for a base hit. Dean turned and looked at his manager, who was furious with Dizzy.

"I guess you're right," Dizzy called. "I was just beginning to think this guy couldn't hit nothing at all!"

Then in 1935 a great change came over Greenberg. "I became a real ballplayer overnight," Hank said. "Early in the season I worried as I always did about having to go up to hit with men on bases. I was afraid I would strike out and the crowd would start booing me. But after a while I started to hit pretty well. And then one day I came out of the dugout and I felt I could hit any pitcher in the world.

" 'Get on base and I'll knock you in,' I hollered to the man at bat.

"Sure enough, he doubled, and a moment later I singled to drive him home. That was the moment I knew I really had become a big league ballplayer."

Hank went on to lead the league in runs batted in that season and hit 36 home runs to tie for the homer title. Mainly because of his slugging, the Tigers won the pennant and their first World Championship. When the season was over, Greenberg received one of baseball's greatest honors by being voted the Most Valuable Player in the American League.

But there were still many thrills ahead for the big slugger. In 1938 he enjoyed one of the finest seasons any player has ever had. The Yankees, however, were great that year and won the pennant easily. Only Hank Greenberg kept the fans interested in what was going on in the American League. He hit home runs at a terrific pace. By the first of September he had hit 46 homers, and the fans were cheering for him to tie Babe Ruth's record of 60 for a season.

For a while it seemed that Greenberg might break the record. He hit ten more home runs to give him a total of 56 with a week of the season still to play. On September 27, playing against the St. Louis Browns, Hank hit two tremendous home runs into the center-field stands at Detroit. It was the eleventh time during the 1938 season that he had hit two home runs in a single game. This was a new major league record. Now he had 58 home runs—only two short of the Babe's record.

At bat against the Chicago White Sox in a 1938 game.

But opposing teams were pitching very carefully to Hank. They would not give him a good ball to hit. On the last day of the season, Hank still needed two homers to tie the Babe's record. He was running out of time—and luck. The Tigers were playing Cleveland in a doubleheader. In the first game, Bobby Feller pitched for Cleveland. His fast ball was overpowering that day. He struck out 18 batters, and Hank could not get his bat around in time to hit any home runs.

The second game was heartbreaking for Hank. In those days the big league teams did not have lights in their ball parks. It was getting dark, and the players could hardly see the ball. The umpires, like everybody else, were rooting for Hank to hit his home runs, but after six innings the field was in partial darkness.

"I'm sorry, Hank," the umpire behind home plate said, "but this is as far as I can go."

"That's all right," Greenberg said. "This is as far as I can go too."

The game was halted because of darkness.

Hank, however, could be proud of his record. He was now the highest paid player in the game. Fans from all over the league came to see this big right-handed slugger hit home runs, just as they had come out to see Babe Ruth. Yet, despite his fame, Greenberg remained the same modest young man who had worked so hard to become a big league first baseman.

In 1940 the Tigers thought they had a chance to win the pennant again. They had Greenberg, of course. They also had a hard-hitting young player named Rudy York. The Tigers knew that with both Greenberg and York in the line-up they would have a powerful attack. They tried to make a catcher out of York, but he was not very good behind the plate. Then they tried to make an outfielder out of him, but he was not very good there either. The only position York could play was first base.

It is not very often that a great player who has made a name for himself at one position will agree to give it up for a younger player. But that is exactly what Greenberg did. For the good of the team he gave up playing first base, a position which had been so difficult for him to master. During spring training he bought himself a fielder's glove, and went out and learned to play left field.

Hank's sacrifice brought another world championship to Detroit. He and York formed a powerful "one-two punch" for the Tigers, and they beat out the Yankees and the Indians for the pennant. Hank batted .340 and led the league in home runs and runs batted in. Once more he was honored by being voted the Most Valuable Player in the American League.

Greenberg crosses the plate, making the first score in the 1940 World Series (which the Tigers won).

Then, at the peak of his career, Greenberg was called away for duty in the Army. Early in 1941 he became the first outstanding player to be drafted. Although the United States was not yet at war, and Greenberg would lose a large salary if he did not play, he went into the Army without a complaint.

"My country comes first," Hank told the newspapermen.

At the time he believed he would lose only one season from baseball. But at the end of 1941 the Japanese attacked the United States Navy at Pearl Harbor, and America began the long and bitter struggle of World War II. Hank served with distinction in the Army Air Forces, flying dangerous missions in Asia and rising from private to captain. But it seemed that his baseball career was over. How could an athlete, nearly 35 years old, return to play championship baseball after having been away from the game for almost five seasons?

The war ended during the summer of 1945. The big leagues had managed to keep going by using players who were either too young or too old to serve in the armed forces. Close pennant races created excitement that season, and the Tigers were right in the thick of the American League race.

Then one day the newspapers headlined the

Catcher Warren Rosar is out by a step as first base-
man Hank Greenberg (5) helps defeat the Athletics
in the final game of a 1946 four game series.

dramatic story: "GREENBERG RETURNS!" Since
Hank had been the first famous ballplayer to be
drafted, he was one of the first to be released from
the armed services. Although the Tigers welcomed

him as an old friend, no one knew whether he would still be able to hit a baseball after all those years.

But Hank had kept himself in good physical condition. He worked out with the team for a few days, and then told them he was ready to play. In the first game, Hank stepped to the plate and walloped a home run!

Now the Tigers were sure they were going to win. They battled the Washington Senators through the closing weeks of the season. Greenberg played an important part in their drive. The race was still close on the last day of the season when the Tigers played the Browns. It was a hard-fought game with the score still tied in the ninth inning. The excitement in the ball park rose to fever pitch as the Tigers filled the bases and Greenberg came to bat. The pitcher threw and Hank, swinging, hit a long home run to win the game and the pennant.

Many a young player would have felt his knees knocking together with fright at the thought of such a dramatic moment. But Hank Greenberg, who once had felt the same way, could scarcely wait to walk up to the plate. He had become a true big leaguer ten years earlier.

JOE DiMAGGIO

In the spring of 1936 the whole baseball world was talking about a young man who had never seen a major league ball park. Although this young man had a "trick knee"—an injury so serious that no one knew whether or not he could play a single game once he arrived in the major leagues—he was on his way to the majors with more publicity than any rookie had ever received before.

"You don't have to worry about this fellow," said a scout who had seen him play in the minor leagues. "He's a *great* ballplayer."

The scout was talking about Joe DiMaggio, a young Italian outfielder from San Francisco. Joe was the son of a fisherman, and several of his older brothers were ballplayers. There were no big league teams on the West Coast in those days. Joe's older brother, Vince, played for the minor league team in San Francisco. But when Joe showed up for a tryout, he was so good that the team sold Vince and put Joe in center field in his place. Soon Joe became the outstanding player in the minor leagues. All the big league teams wanted to buy him from San Francisco.

Then, one day, Joe stepped out of an automobile and something happened to his knee. "It popped like a pistol," he said later. "The pain was terrific and I could hardly stand up. I went to a doctor that night and he told me I had pulled a lot of tendons. It bothered me for a long while."

Joe's knee bothered a lot of the major league scouts, too. Many young players never recover from a serious knee injury, and the scouts soon lost interest in DiMaggio. All the scouts, that is, except those who worked for the Yankees. They decided to take a chance on him. They bought Joe's contract from San Francisco, and told him to report to the Yankees' training camp in Florida in the spring of 1936.

There was much excitement in the Yankee camp that spring. Babe Ruth had retired from baseball. Lou Gehrig was still a great player, but the Yankees needed more than one great player to bring them back to the top of the league.

Everyone was eager to see if DiMaggio was as good as the people in California claimed. And, if he was that good, did he have the courage to come back and play championship baseball after his serious knee injury?

The rookie who arrived at the Yankee camp was a tall, slender young man, 21 years old. He smiled readily, but he was very shy and he seldom spoke to anyone. When he stepped on the playing field, however, he was the center of attention. A right-handed batter, he stood at the plate with his feet spread wide, and stepped into each pitch with a graceful, powerful swing. He was just as impressive when he took his position in the outfield. There has never been a more graceful outfielder, or one who could make difficult catches look so easy. He ranged over the outfield with long strides, pulling in fly balls wherever they were hit. And he threw the ball back to the infield as if he had a cannon hidden up his sleeve.

There was no doubt that DiMaggio was going to be a star. He joined Gehrig and Bill Dickey, the hard-hitting catcher, in creating another "Murderers' Row" for the Yankees. Some people, it is true, sneered at the Yankees for a while. "Just a bunch of window breakers," they called this team. They meant that the Yankees had nothing to offer but a collection of big strong fellows who, with their long drives, could break windows in buildings across the street from the ball parks. But DiMaggio proved the Yankees could do more than that. Time after time he made marvelous catches to rob enemy hitters of base hits. And when enemy runners tried to take an extra base, Joe would cut them down with his powerful, accurate throws.

No other team stood a chance against the Yankees. A pitcher would seem to be getting along fine for a few innings, but soon Gehrig, or DiMaggio, or Dickey would hit a pitch right out of the park and the Yankees would win another game. A newspaperman wrote this little verse about them:

Ashes to ashes, and dust to dust;
If Gehrig and Dickey don't, DiMaggio must!

Joe became known to the fans as "The Yankee Clipper." In his rookie season he was named to the American League's All Star Team. The next season he led the league in home runs. In 1939 he batted .381 to lead the league. When Gehrig, who was fatally ill, had to leave the Yankees, DiMaggio seemed at times to carry the whole team on his broad shoulders.

In 1940 the Yankees slumped to third place. The fans asked if this wonderful team finally was falling apart. They started slowly again in 1941.

Then something happened that suddenly brought the team to life. On May 15, DiMaggio made one hit in four times at bat against the White Sox. The hit did not seem to mean anything at the time. But then day after day Joe kept slugging the ball. Soon the fans realized that he was coming within range of one of baseball's oldest records.

Forty-four years earlier, "Wee Willie" Keeler had hit safely in 44 straight games. Now DiMaggio closed in on that record. It was easy to see why no one during all the intervening years had come close to hitting in 44 straight games. The pressure on Joe increased every day. The crowd and even the other players were tense through the early innings of every game until DiMaggio made his hit. It seemed as if the fans came out not so much to see who won as to see whether DiMaggio got his daily hit. No one had seen so much attention directed solely at one player since fans had flocked into the ball park to watch the Babe hammer home runs.

On July 1 the Yankees played the Red Sox in a doubleheader at Yankee Stadium. The stands were filled, and many of the people had come from long distances to root for DiMaggio. Joe collected two hits in the first game to tie the old record. Then, as the crowd roared its encouragement, Joe smashed the 44-year-old record with a

At Yankee Stadium, against the Red Sox, DiMaggio

solid hit in the second game. Even the sports writers, who seldom cheer at a ball game, rose to their feet to give this great hitter the applause he had earned.

Day after day, Joe continued to hit. Having broken the old record, he seemed to want to set one of his own, one which *no one* would ever come close to. His batting streak finally ended after he had hit in 56 straight games. It took two sensational plays by the Cleveland third baseman, Kenny Keltner, to hold DiMaggio hitless.

The other Yankees, inspired by Joe's remark-

hits in his 44th straight game.

able record, pulled themselves together and became an outstanding team once more. They won the pennant by 17 games and beat the Dodgers in the World Series.

Though DiMaggio had become the great player his admirers had predicted, he never lost his initial shyness. He was not able to crack jokes in the easy manner of some of his teammates. One day, while listening to the Yankees' humorous pitcher, Vernon "Goofy" Gomez, joking with the other players, DiMaggio turned to a friend and said, "I'd give anything if I could do that."

Joe had few friends among the ballplayers. He lived a lonely life, often eating by himself and then going back to his hotel room.

"Everyone else has a home and a family to go to," Joe once told a newspaperman. "All I've got when I go back to my hotel tonight is an empty room and a box of fresh laundry on the bed."

Although he was shy and kept to himself, Joe was liked and admired by his teammates. They recognized him as something more than a great player. He was also their leader.

Joe receives the award for being the Most Valuable Player in the American League in 1941.

"As long as I can remember," a Yankee pitcher once said, "when the Yankees took the field, they all waited for Joe to make the first move. Nothing was said about this custom, but everybody held back and waited for Joe to lead them out of the dugout."

Like most of the other ballplayers of his time, Joe may have lost several of his best years when he joined the Army during World War II. He was older, of course, when he returned, and he seemed to suffer injuries more often. Still, the Yankees could not win without him. "As DiMag goes, so go the Yankees," the newspapermen liked to say. They were simply stating a fact. When Joe was injured, the Yankees lost. When he was healthy, he was their leader and their star.

Joe had a fine season in 1947, leading the Yankees to the World Championship. In 1948 he suffered from leg injuries, and the Yankees could not win. Joe played as often as he could in order to keep the team in the pennant race. During the closing days of the season, Joe could hardly walk, but he went into the line-up to help the Yankees try to catch up with the Red Sox and Indians. On the next to the last day of the season, he slammed four hits at Boston, but he received little help from his teammates, and the Yankees lost. As he left the field that day, even the Boston fans rose to their feet to give him a long ovation.

The fans knew that Joe's career was drawing to a close. In the spring of 1949, in fact, it seemed to be over. Joe had undergone an operation on his injured foot during the winter. And during spring training he discovered that the injury had not healed properly. Casey Stengel had just become the manager of the Yankees, and he was hoping to win a pennant in his first year at Yankee Stadium. But he knew that without DiMaggio he did not have a chance.

As the team traveled north to open the season, DiMaggio had to tell Stengel he was not able to

Nurse Mary Read inspects the Yankee veteran's bandaged foot after his operation.

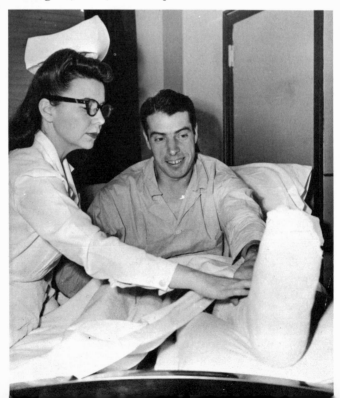

play. The pain in his foot was intense. The Yankees sent him home ahead of the team for further treatment. A foot injury very like DiMaggio's had put an end to Rogers Hornsby's career. Joe feared that his own career was finished too. He had to follow the progress of his teammates from his bed. His foot was too sore to stand on.

Joe's spirits were kept up by the news that the Yankees were doing surprisingly well. They got off to a fast start and took a grip on first place, though no one believed they could stay there. The Red Sox, led by the marvelous Ted Williams, were too powerful. The baseball experts felt that the Yankees, playing without their star, would not be able to hold off the Boston team all season.

Then one day DiMaggio found that the soreness had left his foot. He could stand on it again, and even walk comfortably. He went up to Yankee Stadium, put on his old uniform with the big number 5 on the back, and took batting practice with his teammates.

"How does it feel?" everybody asked him afterward.

"The heel feels fine," Joe told them, grinning. "And so does this uniform. It feels so good I think I'll wear it to bed."

He did not wear it to bed, of course. But every day he went up to the stadium, put it on and practiced with the others. Slowly his strength and

89

his timing began to return.

"When will you put DiMaggio back in the line-up?" the newspapermen asked manager Stengel. "I won't use him until he's ready to play," Stengel said. "I want all of Joe, or nothing."

Soon afterward the Yankees got ready to leave for Boston, where they would play an important three-game series with the Red Sox. The Red Sox were catching up fast now. They were determined to beat the Yankees two or three times and take over first place for themselves. It was then that DiMaggio told Stengel he was ready to play.

The Boston fans were rooting hard for their own team. But when DiMaggio came to bat in the first inning they cheered him for his courage. Joe lined a single to left field, and scored the Yankees' first run a few moments later. In the third inning Joe came to bat again, this time with a runner on base. He waited for the pitch, timed it perfectly, and drove it into the screen above the left-field wall for his first home run of the season.

The Red Sox fought back. In the ninth inning they put the tying run on base and Ted Williams came to bat. It began to look as if DiMaggio's great effort would be wiped out. Williams, swinging hard, slammed the ball to deep center field. But DiMaggio, gliding back gracefully, caught the ball for the final out.

DiMaggio starts his first American League game of 1949 with a hit.

"I'm glad the Red Sox didn't tie it up," Joe said later in the dressing room. "I was so tired I couldn't play another inning."

In the second game of the series, the Red Sox started to hit the ball as everybody had expected them to. They pounded the Yankee pitchers and built up a 7–1 lead. Then DiMaggio came to bat in the fifth inning and hit a home run with two runners on base, putting the Yankees back in the game. Finally they tied the score and DiMag came to bat again, this time in the eighth inning. Again, Joe timed the pitch perfectly and slammed a long home run to win the game for the Yankees.

The whole country was talking about DiMaggio. Just as the Yankees had seemed about to drop out of first place, Joe had come out of the hospital to put new life into them. The Yankees had stunned the Red Sox twice, and it was DiMaggio who had delivered the hardest blows. Now the two teams met in the final game of the series.

It was a pitchers' duel for seven innings. The Yankees led, 3–2, but the Red Sox were still dangerous. Then, in the eighth inning, DiMaggio came to bat with two runners on base. The Red Sox pitcher, Mel Parnell, worked carefully on Joe. The count went to three balls and two strikes. Parnell came in with the next pitch and Joe pounded it into the light tower on top of the left-field wall for his longest home run of the series. That was the winning blow. The Red Sox got one more run, but the Yankees won the game, 6–3. Boston's drive had been turned back. The Yankees went on to win the pennant and the World Series. When it was all over they could look back to that dramatic series in Boston and say that it was the turning point in their fortunes.

Once again the newspapers told the story: "As DiMag goes, so go the Yankees!"

TED WILLIAMS

It was a wild and exciting day at Fenway Park, the home of the Boston Red Sox. The fans who crowded the old ball park on that midsummer day in 1946 cheered the slightest move made by the players. They had a right to be excited—and proud too. Baseball's All Star Game was being played at Fenway Park for the first time. And the Red Sox, who were the hosts for the game, were on their way to their first pennant in 28 years. In fact, the American League squad was dominated by Boston players.

The National League All Stars did not have a chance. The American League's pitching was almost perfect. And when the American League took its turn at bat, Ted Williams blasted the game apart. The only time the National League pitchers stopped Ted was when they walked him. When they pitched to him, Fenway Park rang with the sound of bat striking ball. In the early innings, Williams slammed two singles and a home run as the American League built up a commanding lead.

The Boston fans gave Williams a mighty cheer when he came to bat for the last time that afternoon. Rip Sewell, an experienced pitcher, was on the mound for the National League. Rip had a "trick pitch," which he threw only once in a great while, but when he threw it he usually fooled the batter. He called the pitch his "blooper ball." He pretended he was going to throw a fast ball but then, at the last minute, he simply lobbed the pitch high in the air. The batter usually stood there in surprise. If he did swing at it, his timing was off and he could not hit it solidly.

But Ted Williams was a different sort of hitter. He waited at the plate for Sewell's "blooper" to drop out of the sky, adjusted his swing to meet the ball squarely, and hit a towering home run. The American League won the game, 12–0, and afterward everyone was talking about Williams.

"That was the greatest exhibition of hitting I have ever seen," one big league manager said the next day. "Williams is fantastic!"

No finer natural hitter than Williams has ever

come to the big leagues. He had the power of
Babe Ruth and the keen batting eye of Rogers
Hornsby. Only Joe DiMaggio in his own time
rivaled him for the honor of being the greatest
player in the game. Yet DiMaggio somehow was
an inspiration to his teammates, and led them to
victory time and again. Williams did not have this
quality. He could not control himself, much less
lead other men, and as a result the Red Sox saw
few triumphs during his long career in Boston.

The 1946 All Star Game was typical of Wil-

Ted Williams of the Red Sox and Joe DiMaggio,
Yankee star, rest their feet after their victory in the
1946 All Star Game.

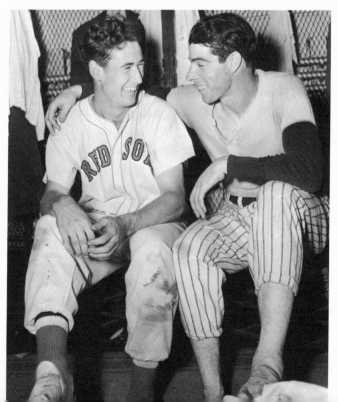

liams' career. Although All Star games are colorful spectacles, bringing together the best players in each league, they are actually exhibition games. An exhibition does not count in the standings, and it makes little difference—except for the pride of the individual players—who wins the game.

Williams was at his best in games of this sort. When he was smashing the ball into the seats during pre-game, home-run-hitting contests, or in All Star Games and other exhibitions, Williams could not be matched by any other hitter who ever lived. But in an important game the story was often different. Ted hit a number of game-winning home runs, of course. A hitter with his ability could not help but get hits in important games. But, on the whole, many players with less natural talent have in the long run proved to be more valuable to their teams.

Right from the start, Williams was clearly an extraordinary hitter. Like so many other sluggers, he began his career as a pitcher. But scouts who saw him in San Diego, his home town, liked his power at the plate better than his pitching arm. In 1939, when Ted came to the Red Sox at the age of 20, he already had gained the reputation that would stay with him throughout his career. No one doubted that he was a great hitter. No one doubted, either, that his frequent sulks would give the Red Sox many unhappy moments.

As a rookie, Ted hit 31 home runs and batted .327. He added terrific power to what was already a strong batting order at Boston. He had a remarkable pair of eyes. Other players told how he could read the numbers on the license plates of automobiles far ahead of his own car when the other people in the car could make out only the outline of the plates.

He was sensitive in other ways too. A player told of a visit he had made with Williams to a factory where bats were manufactured. The firm's president asked Ted what he thought of the bats that were lying on a special rack.

"This one on the right is a little heavier," Ted said after he had lifted each of them.

"No, it's not," the manufacturer said. "Those bats are all made to the same specifications. They're all exactly the same."

But when Williams insisted that one was heavier than the others, the manufacturer ordered each of the bats to be weighed. Williams was right! The bat he had singled out weighed a quarter of an ounce more than the others.

Ted devoted all his time to improving his hitting. "All I want out of life," he said, "is to be able to walk down the street and have people point to me and say 'There goes the greatest hitter who ever lived.'"

The Red Sox found that Williams could win a

ball game all by himself with his bat. But, if he was sulking, he could hurt the team, too. On those days he seemed to play half-heartedly. Fly balls dropped in front of him in the outfield. He showed little interest in running the bases. Joe Cronin, the Red Sox manager, put in a pinch runner for Ted one day during his rookie season.

"Ted," Cronin told him, "you're a boy playing a man's game. And if you're going to stay in baseball, you've got to be a man."

Although the Red Sox fined Williams several times for his half-hearted playing, Ted never "grew up." He had what the players called "rabbit ears." They were very sensitive to insults from spectators or opposing players. If he chased a fly ball at half speed and it fell safely in front of him, the crowds would begin to boo him and shout insults. This made Ted furious. It got so that when he hit a home run and the crowd cheered him, he refused to tip his cap as the other players did. He was so determined to be the best player that even the smallest criticism upset him. And then he would very nearly become the *worst* player.

Ted never seemed to be able to keep his mouth shut at a time when silence would have helped him. Once, when he was especially upset about some name the fans had called him, or some criticism the reporters had leveled at him, he remarked that it wasn't such a splendid thing to be a ballplayer after all.

"I'd rather be a fireman," he said.

It was an unfortunate remark. The fans used to jeer at him: "Fireman, save my child!" When Ted came to bat against the White Sox, all the Chicago players in their dugout put on firemen's hats and one of them sounded a loud siren. Ted was angrier than ever!

Ted had his finest season in 1941. He hit a home run to win the All Star Game in the ninth inning. Coming down to the final day of the

The Boston Howitzer crosses the plate after hitting the home run that won the 1941 All Star Game in the ninth inning.

season Ted was batting .400. There was considerable excitement because baseball had not had a .400 hitter in more than ten years, and the fans were beginning to think that no one would ever hit that high again. The Red Sox closed their season with a doubleheader at Philadelphia. Since they had dropped out of the pennant race early in the season, there was no reason to put their best players on the field for these meaningless games. If Williams did not play that day, he would be sure to finish the season with a .400 average. If he did play, he might not get any hits and his average would drop below .400.

"Do you want to sit out today's games?" manager Cronin asked him. •

Williams shook his head. "I'm playing," he said. "If I'm going to be champion, I want to win like a champion."

He did. In the first game he pounded three singles and a home run. He came back to play in the second game and hit a single and a double. His six hits for the afternoon gave him a final average of .406. Baseball has not had a .400 hitter since.

Like DiMaggio and Greenberg, Williams fought for his country during World War II. Being younger than they, he was still at the very peak of his career when he returned in 1946. The Red Sox won the pennant that year—the only time during Ted's years in Boston. They had a powerful team, with such sluggers as Rudy York and Bobby Doerr joining Williams in the batting order. Ted was really on top that season. His tremendous exhibition of hitting ruined the National League in the All Star Game. And the Red Sox trampled on the other American League teams as Boston drew closer to the pennant. It seemed as if Williams might break a number of batting records.

Then a strange thing happened. One day when the Red Sox played the Cleveland Indians, Ted came to bat and the entire Cleveland team went into the "Boudreau Shift." This was a plan devised by the Indians' manager, Lou Boudreau. He knew that Williams was always trying to pull the ball to right field in order to hit home runs.

So Boudreau moved most of his players to the right side of the field. The rightfielder played almost on the foul line. The first baseman did the same, stationing himself deep behind the bag. The second baseman played close to first base, and the shortstop came over to the other side of the bag, standing where the second baseman usually played. The third baseman stood behind second base. The center fielder moved into the usual position of the right fielder. And the left fielder moved in close to the infield, just behind the shortstop's normal position.

Such an outlandish defensive shift would not have been possible against other great hitters. They simply would have bunted along the third-base line, or punched the ball over the left fielder's head. But Boudreau knew exactly how Williams would react to the shift.

"I wanted to hit a homer more than ever," Williams said, "just so I could tell Boudreau, 'You put them in the right position all right, but you should have had taller men!' "

Boudreau had *dared* him to punch the ball to left field, but Ted would not do it. The shift made him so angry that he tried to hit the ball *over* everybody's head and into the right-field stands. For a while Williams had some success against the shift. But many of the line drives he hit—which normally would have fallen safely for hits—were caught by one of the players standing near the foul line.

"If they had used that shift against me," Ty Cobb told a newspaperman, "I would have batted 1.000. I'd have stopped it fast by hitting everything to left field. Tell Ted what I said the next time you see him."

But it was very difficult to tell Williams anything. He went on hitting just the way he pleased. His batting average dropped a little during the rest of the season. His fast start, however, helped him put together a fine record that

On September 28, 1960, Ted Williams hit the 521st homer of his long career.

year. He batted .342, hit 38 home runs and batted in 123 runs. He was voted the Most Valuable Player in the American League.

But Ted came to grief in his only World Series. The Red Sox played the Cardinals that fall. Knowing how successful the Boudreau Shift had been against Williams, the Cardinals used a shift of their own. Ted managed to get only five hits —all singles—in 25 times at bat for a poor average of .200. The Red Sox lost the World Series.

Williams remained a powerful hitter for many years. Certainly no man alive knew more than he about the art of hitting a baseball. Most of the other ballplayers liked Ted because he was very generous about sharing his knowledge with them. When a ballplayer was in a slump, or was having trouble hitting a certain pitch, he would ask Ted about it. Ted always gave good advice, even to players on other teams. When one reporter asked Al Kaline of the Detroit Tigers for the secret of his success as a hitter, Kaline did not hesitate.

"Ted Williams—his advice straightened me out," Kaline said.

Yet Ted was his own worst enemy. He was often in trouble with the Red Sox officials. Once, after he had hit a home run, he turned in the direction of the stands and spit at the crowd. The Red Sox fined him heavily for that unsportsman-like gesture. While Ted went out of his way to do nice things in private for children and handicapped people, he kept up his war against the Boston fans and the newspapermen to the end of his career.

And even beyond! When the Red Sox finally won another pennant, after a gallant fight in 1967, their fans were immensely proud of them. Williams had retired by then, but he was still considered part of the Red Sox "official family," and he served as a batting instructor at their spring training camp. As the Red Sox prepared for the World Series, their fans and their former players flocked to Boston from all over the country to pay tribute to this fighting team. They were all there—except Ted Williams.

Where was he? He went fishing. Ted still preferred to walk his lonely way.

STAN MUSIAL

Sports fans feel sorry for an aging athlete. They can see that his performance on the diamond isn't as good as it once was. He's no longer as indispensable to his team, and it is only a question of time before his playing career will be over. But a star who has played for many years has at least enjoyed considerable fame and has collected memories that will remain with him for the rest of his life. It is much more difficult for a young player to have his career come to an abrupt end before he is even 20 years old.

That was the prospect faced by a young man named Stanley Frank Musial in 1940. He was only 19 years old, yet his dream of a major league career already seemed to be shattered. He had become just another pitcher with a sore arm, whose "future" had vanished almost before it began.

Musial had been an outstanding schoolboy athlete in his home town of Donora, Pennsylvania. One of the best high school basketball players in his part of the state, he was best known as a left-handed pitcher. In one game he struck out 13 batters in six innings. Major league scouts began to follow him around. One of them, a scout for the St. Louis Cardinals, offered Stan a contract.

This was exactly what 17-year-old Stan wanted —a chance at a major league career! But his father, Lukatz Musial, had come to the United States as a poor boy from Poland. He knew the value of an education, and he wanted Stan to have one. He told his son he could not sign a contract with the Cardinals.

Stan was heartbroken. He pleaded with his father to change his mind. Mr. Musial thought about the problem for some time. He realized that he had come to the United States to get away from people who were always telling him what he could and could not do. Why should he stand in the way of what his son wanted to do? It was one of the most exciting days Stan would ever know when his father told him that he could become a professional baseball player.

The Cardinals sent young Musial to the minor

leagues to get more experience. The boy was still wild, as most inexperienced left-handers are, but he showed great promise. He began to dream of pitching in St. Louis one day. Stan was a good hitter too. When he was not pitching, his manager let him play the outfield.

Then one day in 1940 disaster struck. Stan was playing the outfield for Daytona Beach in the Florida State League. He raced in to try to make a running catch and, diving for the ball, rolled over on his left shoulder. He made the catch, but at the same time he felt a sharp pain in his shoulder. The next day he could hardly throw a ball. Slowly the awful truth began to dawn on young Stanley Frank Musial—at the age of 19 he had a "dead" arm. His career as a pitcher was over.

Stan could not think about going back to Donora and starting his education again. He had a wife and child to support. Luckily, he found a friend just when he needed one most. The manager of the minor league team for which Stan had been playing was Dickie Kerr. Kerr had been a big league pitcher many years before. He did not give up hope for Stan's career.

"Don't worry about looking for a job right now," Kerr told Musial. "Why don't you and your family move in with Mrs. Kerr and me? That will save you a lot of worrying." Since Stan had already showed that he was a good hitter,

Kerr was going to try to make an outfielder out of him.

So Musial, like Ruth, Gehrig and Williams, left the pitcher's mound to try to make good as a hitter. For Stan the change was difficult at first. His arm was still weak, and an outfielder needs a strong arm. But Kerr worked patiently with him, and the strength slowly returned to his left arm. Stan finished the season as an outfielder, batting .311.

The next spring Musial reported with some of the other good young minor league players owned by the Cardinals to their training camp in Florida. Branch Rickey, who ran the Cardinals, looked over each of the young players carefully. One youngster caused him to take a second look. He was a left-handed batter who stood at the plate in a curious crouch. His feet were close together, his knees were bent and his bat was cocked straight up and down behind his left ear. Strangest of all was his habit of peering just over his right shoulder at the pitcher.

Rickey looked up the young man's name and background in the team's files. "Why, this boy is listed as a pitcher," Rickey said. "He's not a *pitcher*. He's a *hitter!*"

Some of the baseball men who saw Musial and his strange stance at the plate were not quite so sure. They had never seen anything like it before.

Rookie outfielder Stan Musial.

As a big league pitcher said later, "Musial looks
like a kid peeking around a corner to see if the
cops are coming."

But Rickey, a shrewd baseball man, had seen
something in Stan's "corkscrew" stance. "No batter's correctness of form is determined by the position he gets into before the ball is pitched," Rickey

said. "When the ball leaves the pitcher's hand, that is the time you take a picture of a batsman to determine the correctness of his form. When the ball is pitched Stan takes his true position. He is no longer in a crouch and his bat is held back and so steady a coin wouldn't fall off the end of it. Then he takes the proper stride and the level swing. His batting form is ideal."

Rickey was right. This determined young man, who had supposedly been "finished" as a ballplayer only the season before, would move to the major leagues with dramatic speed. The Cardinals sent him to Springfield at the beginning of the 1941 season. During his short stay in Springfield, Stan batted .379 and led the league in home runs. The Cardinals quickly promoted him to their top farm team at Rochester. There he kept right on hammering the ball, batting .326. Everybody who watched Stan in the minors raved about his skill with a bat in his hands, so the Cardinals brought him to St. Louis for the last two weeks of the season.

Stan played his first big-league game against the Boston Braves. The Braves' pitcher was a veteran named Jim Tobin, whose knuckle balls were very difficult for young players to hit. The first time Musial swung at one of those knucklers, he popped it up. But the next time at bat, Stan was ready for the pitch. His timing was perfect and he drove the ball against the right-field wall for a double. A few innings later, he got another hit.

Casey Stengel, who managed the Braves in those days, was impressed by the number of good young players the Cardinals were bringing to the major leagues. But Musial stood out, even among the other talented players. Stengel shook his head in wonderment.

"Those Cardinals got another good one," he said to a friend.

Stan played 12 games for the Cardinals at the

Musial slides safely into third in the fourth game of the 1942 World Series.

end of that 1941 season, and batted .426. He had established himself as the outstanding young player in the National League. As Stengel had said, "The Cardinals got another good one."

Stan became the difference between victory and defeat for the Cardinals. In 1942 he batted .315 to lead them to the first of three consecutive pennants. In the World Series, he proved that Dickie Kerr's patience in converting him to an outfielder in the minor leagues had not been wasted. Stan made a couple of sensational catches to halt rallies by the Yankees and win the world championship for the Cardinals.

In 1943, Stan won the first of his seven batting championships with a .357 average. He batted .347 in 1944 as he led the Cardinals to another world championship. In 1945 Stan served in the United States armed forces. The Cardinals, to no one's surprise, did not win the pennant that year.

Stan returned to his greatest triumphs after World War Two. It was as if he had never been away. His .365 batting average led the league in 1946 and the Cardinals won the pennant and the World Series. Stan was voted the Most Valuable Player in the National League.

Despite his success and his fame, Stan remained the most likable of ballplayers. He did not demand the special privileges which Ted Williams and

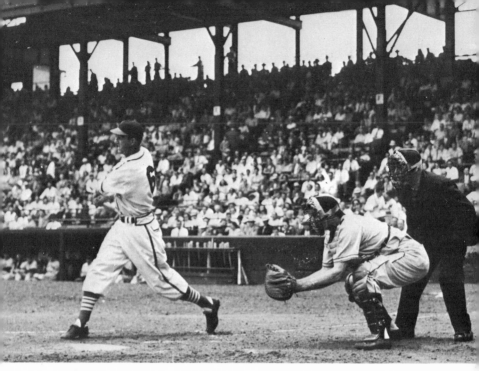

When he returned from the armed forces, Stan hit the ball as if he had never been away.

other stars had wanted. He remained "one of the boys." He sat in the back of the bus with the rookies on the way to the ball park. He did not try to squeeze in extra batting practice at the expense of some unknown players. And he was never too busy to talk to a fan or a newspaperman.

"Do you have any enemies?" Harry Caray, the Cardinals' radio and television announcer, once asked Stan.

"I hope not," Musial answered. "I try to treat people the way I'd want to be treated."

Stan did not forget his old friends. As soon as

he began earning a large salary, he bought a house for Dickie Kerr, the minor league manager who had once been so good to him. Being the sort of man he was, Musial did not want the news of this good deed to get in the newspapers. But somebody told the whole story of his generosity. Stan, of course, was very embarrassed, and pretended that it was not such a great thing after all.

Perhaps one of Stan's teammates said it best. "When my son grows up," this player said, "I can tell him I played with Stan Musial. It was a thrill, an honor and a pleasure."

National League pitchers, of course, did not get a great deal of pleasure out of pitching to Stan. They were the only people in the world he abused, and he was very hard on them indeed. A pitcher could not count on getting Stan out even when he was injured. In 1948, while Musial was playing against the Braves, his wrists were so sore and swollen that he could not snap his swing.

"The pain in my wrists was so bad that I made up my mind I wasn't going to waste any swings," Stan said. "I swung at the ball only five times all day, and I made five hits."

Musial was not supposed to be a home-run hitter, but in 1948 he hit 39 homers.

"I never once took deliberate aim at the fences," Stan said later. "So I asked myself, 'If you can hit 39 homers without trying for even one, how many

could you hit if you were *trying* to hit home runs?'
So the next season I began trying for a home run
every time up. By the middle of the season I'd hit
only about a dozen homers, and my average was
barely over .300. Not only had I stopped hitting
homers, I'd stopped hitting singles. So that's when
I made up my mind to just go up there and meet
the ball like I'd always done before."

Stan was tough wherever he played, but he was
especially great in New York. In those days the

*Musial hits a home run against the Giants at the
Polo Grounds.*

National League had two teams in New York City —the New York Giants and the Brooklyn Dodgers. Stan used to tear them apart. One day Willard Mullin, the sports cartoonist, drew a cartoon showing a Giant and a Dodger taking Musial to the railroad station. They were rushing him along toward the train, carrying his bags and patting him on the back.

"Hurry up, Stan," one of them was saying. "We wouldn't want you to miss your train."

"Have a nice trip," the other one was saying, "and don't hurry back."

Stan hit five home runs in one day against the Giants—two in one game of a doubleheader, and three in the other. Brooklyn fans hated to see him come to bat against the Dodgers when there were runners on base. He was sure to drive them home. One day as Stan came to bat with runners on base, a Brooklyn fan put his head in his hands and moaned:

"Oh-oh! Here comes that *man* again!"

After that the fans and writers began calling Musial—"Stan the Man."

Stan holds more records than any other player in the history of the National League. He hit six home runs in All Star Games. One of them put a dramatic end to the 1955 All Star Game in the twelfth inning. Of all Musial's records, he is probably the proudest of his final total of 3,630 base hits, a record for National Leaguers, and second only to the 4,191 hits collected by Ty Cobb in the American League. But when he was once asked what his greatest thrill in baseball had been, Stan said with his usual humility: "Every time I put on a Cardinal uniform."

Musial took off that uniform for the last time at the end of the 1963 season. No one who saw it ever will forget Stan's last game. The fans, his teammates and his friends gave him one of the most heart-warming celebrations in the history of baseball. They showered him with gifts, and announced that a huge statue of Stan would be erected in St. Louis.

"Gosh," Stan said, "they should wait till I'm dead first."

Then he went out and played his last game, banging Jim Maloney of the Reds for two hits. After the game, one of the reporters asked Stan if he had wanted to hit a home run that day.

"I was always a singles hitter," Stan said. "This was the way to end it."

Everyone in baseball felt something had gone out of the game when he retired. "The only thing I have against baseball," said Al Kaline of the Detroit Tigers, "is not getting the opportunity to watch Stan Musial in more than a few games. Stan is a true symbol of what baseball would like all players to be."

WILLIE MAYS

Willie Mays was having a wonderful time. He was playing for the Giants' minor league team at Minneapolis early in the 1951 season. Playing? . . . He was tearing the league apart. After 35 games he was batting .477. The fans in Minneapolis had never seen anything like Willie. He was having great fun—and getting paid for it too!

One night Willie went to the movies. He was enjoying the picture, just as he enjoyed everything in those days, when somebody came over to him and said the team's manager wanted to talk to him back at the hotel. Willie left the theater to find out what the trouble was.

"Pack your bags, Willie," the manager said. "The Giants want you to report to them right away."

"Me? Going to the big leagues?" Willie asked in astonishment. "Why, I ain't *ready* for that big league pitching!"

It is easy to understand Willie's astonishment at that moment. Everything had happened so fast. Only a year or so earlier he had been playing sandlot baseball back in Alabama, just as his father had done as a young man. Then a scout for the Giants had signed Willie, and he had gone off to play minor league ball. Now, at the age of 20, he was being told to report to the Giants at the Polo Grounds in New York, where they used to play their games.

For a while Willie thought he had been right to protest that he wasn't ready for big league ball. He went 12 times at bat for the Giants before he got a hit. But his first hit was one to remember! It came against Warren Spahn, one of the craftiest pitchers in baseball. Willie hit the ball onto the roof of the left-field stands for a tremendous home run.

Then came another hitless stretch. Willie was unsure of himself. When several of the older players kidded him about not getting any hits, he began to think he wasn't wanted on the team. One day Leo Durocher, the Giants' manager, walked into the clubhouse and found Willie sitting in front of his locker, with tears in his eyes.

"What's the matter, Willie?" Durocher asked.

"Mr. Durocher, I can't hit this good pitching," Willie sobbed. "You'd better send me back where I came from."

Durocher put an arm around Willie's shoulder. "Willie," he said, "you're not going *anywhere*. You're my center fielder."

This moment was the turning point in Mays' young career. Now that the manager had told him he was wanted on the Giants, Willie regained his confidence. Playing baseball was fun once more. And it became fun for all the other players on the

Manager Leo Durocher (left) with super-rookie Willie Mays in 1951.

team. Willie had so much energy and he laughed so often that he made even the older players feel as if they were kids again.

"Say, hey!" Willie would shout in his high-pitched voice.

And all the other players took up the cry: "Say, hey!" Willie soon became known around the Polo Grounds as "The Say-Hey Kid."

Everyone who saw him knew that Willie Mays was going to be a great ballplayer. But it was as a center fielder that he first began to excite the crowds. He had terrific running speed and he roamed about in his position as few players had done before him. He made amazing catches in the deepest parts of the outfield. When he caught the ball, he showed the other teams that he had the strongest throwing arm in baseball. His throws came back to the infield as if they were shot from a rifle, and enemy runners trying to take an extra base were cut down time after time.

Willie also had that rare ability to make even the easy plays look exciting. If a batter hit a fly ball to short center field, Willie would scamper in, losing his cap on the way. Then he would settle down under the ball, tap his glove with his bare hand, and cup his two hands right at his belt buckle. The ball would plop into his glove, and the fans would cheer him for his "basket catch."

For a while Mays struck out often. Experi-

Outfielder Mays slides safely back to first on an attempted pick-off by the Chicago Cubs.

enced pitchers were able to fool him when he came to bat. Even a catcher was able to fool Willie. Roy Campanella, the Dodgers' catcher, was one of the most famous players of his time. Willie had heard all about Campy, of course, and he was very impressed when Campy went out of his way to be nice to him. Every time Willie went to bat against the Dodgers, Campy would begin a conversation with him.

"Yes, Mr. Campanella," Willie would say politely. "No, Mr. Campanella."

Finally it dawned on Willie that he was spending so much of his time at bat answering Campy's questions that he was not hitting the Dodgers' pitchers. Willie had learned something new about baseball.

"Let me be, Mr. Campanella," Willie would say after that. "I got to concentrate on my *hitting.*"

Pretty soon Willie was recognized as one of the most dangerous young hitters in the league. His teammates, inspired by his enthusiasm, began to play winning baseball. In August of 1951 they were in second place, 13½ games behind the Dodgers. Then, led by Mays, they began to creep up. When the Giants needed the big play to win a game—a home run, a great catch, or a strong throw—Willie gave it to them.

The Giants overtook the Dodgers on the final

weekend of the season, tying them for first place. Then they beat the Dodgers in a play-off to win the pennant.

"The spark was Mays," manager Durocher said after the season. "When it looked like we couldn't win, he carried us on his back. He carried the whole darn team on his back!"

The Giants got a bad break the next season. Their great young player, Willie Mays, was drafted into the Army. For two years they struggled along without him. Then, in 1954, the newspapers told the story in their headlines:

WILLIE MAYS COMES BACK

Willie rejoined the Giants at their spring training camp and once again his teammates heard the cry: "Say, hey!" He had been a fine player when he left for the Army, but he was a great one when he returned. With Willie in the line-up, the Giants were happy and confident. When they got into trouble, they looked to their center fielder to set matters right again, just as he had three years earlier. Mays hit 41 home runs, drove in 110 runs and led the league with a batting average of .345.

The Giants won the pennant and then bowled over the Cleveland Indians in four straight games in the World Series. One of the highlights of the series was Willie's great catch of a tremendous drive hit by Vic Wertz to the center-field wall.

After the season, Willie was voted the Most Valuable Player in the National League.

Everybody liked to talk to Willie, just as he liked to talk to them. He was always full of fun. "Can you spot a spit ball when it's on the way to the plate?" a newspaperman asked him.

"Sure," Willie told him. "But I always wait till it spins so I can hit it on the dry side."

Sometimes Willie's sense of humor got him into trouble. One day he singled against the Cincinnati Reds. The Reds' first baseman was Ted Kluszewski, a giant of a man whose arms were so big they looked like tree trunks. Willie bent down and picked up a handful of dirt, as the ballplayers usually do when they are on base. Holding the dirt in their hands helps them to keep a closed fist so fielders won't step on their fingers if they have to slide. After every pitch, the base runner usually drops his handful of dirt, then scoops up some more.

But instead of dropping the dirt on the ground, Willie sneaked up behind Kluszewski, who was covering first base, and poured the dirt into his hip pocket. On the next pitch, Willie did the same thing. Klu did not say anything until Willie put his foot on the bag. Then Klu lifted his own huge foot and clamped it down on Willie's. Everyone in the ball park could hear Willie's high-pitched howl.

"Get off my foot, Klu!" Willie screamed.

"Are you finished fooling around?" Klu asked.

"Yep," Willie answered hastily.

And Kluszewski released his foot.

When the Giants left New York and moved into their new stadium in San Francisco, Willie went right on slugging the ball. Of course, once in a while he fell into a slump, just like anyone else. One year when he was in an especially bad slump, he walked up to the batting cage during practice. He noticed that the player who was already in the cage slammed a couple of balls over the fence.

"Looks like a good bat," Willie said.

"Want to try it?" the other player asked as he came out of the batting cage.

Willie nodded. "I can't do no worse," he said.

He used the bat during practice, and it felt good to him. So he used it during the game—and walloped four home runs!

If some fans got the idea that Willie's high spirits on the field meant that he did not care very much about what happened, they were mistaken. Mays is a great player because he concentrates on every pitch, just as Ty Cobb and Rogers Hornsby did. At times he has played the game so hard he has collapsed from exhaustion. One day he came to bat during a doubleheader, and fainted at the plate. But he returned to action every time after a brief rest.

*At San Francisco, Willie Mays went right on slugging
the ball.*

By 1965 the fans began to realize that Willie was the greatest home-run hitter in the history of the National League. Only one National Leaguer had ever-hit more home runs than Willie, and that was Mel Ott, who also had played for the Giants. Ott finished his career with 511 homers. Willie, who was then 34 years old, slammed 52 home runs in 1965 to bring his lifetime total to 504. After the season, Willie was once more voted the Most Valuable Player in the National League. Then, in 1966, he set out on the trail of Ott's record. Willie tied the record, and then his troubles began as he tried for his 512th homer.

"I never had a chance to brush it off as another home run," Willie told a reporter. "I couldn't forget it because there were dozens of cameramen around me every day, waiting to take a picture of me breaking the record. In a way it got to be funny. Those cameramen were being paid big money to get that picture—about $80 a day—and they weren't in any hurry for me to hit it. In fact, I think they were rooting against me. I got so anxious I couldn't do a thing."

At last Willie hit his 512th homer, and he was a very happy man.

"But I sure didn't enjoy those two weeks when I was trying for it," he said. Then he grinned. "But I guess those cameramen did. I made them all rich!"

Mays signs the ball that gave him his 512th homer—in May of 1966.

Baseball is not Willie's whole life. He also likes to play golf, and he has said more than once that —once his baseball career is over—he would enjoy becoming a professional golfer. And, like so many great players, he has gone out of his way to help young people. Several years ago, Hubert H. Humphrey, who was then the Vice-President of the United States, asked Mays if he would help the government get its Job Corps program established. Willie quickly agreed. He spent a great deal of time visiting Job Corps centers to talk to the young men. And even during the baseball season, Willie gave assistance to the program by publicizing it and recruiting other young men for its centers.

"I only finished high school," he has said. "But today kids need more than just a high school education and skill in playing baseball. They ought to have special training for the good jobs that are around."

Willie is a very fortunate man in that he has been able to earn his living for so many years doing exactly what he likes best—playing baseball. In 1966 he became the highest paid player in baseball history when he signed a two-year contract calling for $130,000 a year. He was then 35 years old, an age when most players are thinking of quitting. But of course Willie Mays is something special. As Leo Durocher said:

"Willie will be playing baseball better than anybody else when he's in a rocking chair."

MICKEY MANTLE

It was a quiet afternoon at Detroit late in the 1968 season. The Yankees were playing the Tigers, who already had clinched the American League pennant. Denny McLain, who recently had become the first big league pitcher in 34 years to win 30 games in a season, was on his way to his 31st victory. After seven innings he was coasting along with a 6–1 lead.

It was not the sort of day to stir excitement among the fans. But the crowd suddenly came to life in the top of the eighth inning. This was the Yankees' final game of the year in Detroit, and when Mickey Mantle walked to the plate the crowd came to its feet to applaud him. Though he often had ruined the Tigers with his mighty home runs, the Detroit fans were showing their appreciation for the many thrills he had given them through the years. Mickey needed only one home run to pass Jimmy Foxx and step into third place on the all-time home-run list, behind Babe Ruth and Willie Mays.

McLain got his first two pitches on the inside corner of the plate. The count on Mantle was no balls and two strikes. Then Mickey made a motion to McLain, telling him to get the ball out over the center of the plate where Mickey could get his bat on it. McLain, far ahead in the game, wound up and threw a fat one right down the middle. Mickey, swinging, drove the ball into the upper deck for the 535th home run of his long career. As he rounded third base, he yelled his thanks to the Detroit pitcher. McLain threw him a salute.

"McLain made me a fan of his for life," Mickey said in the Yankee clubhouse after the game.

Over in the Tiger clubhouse, McLain—who had won the game, 6–2—was asked if he had let Mickey hit the home run.

"Not exactly," McLain replied. But he smiled when he said it. "You know—Mickey was my boyhood idol."

Baseball, as a rule, is a cut-throat game. Players struggle to win games and build up their records. But once in a while the sentiment shows through. It showed through that afternoon in Detroit when

*Mickey Mantle rounds the bases after hitting his
535th homer at Detroit in August of 1968.*

a young pitcher just reaching stardom made a gallant gesture toward an aging player who was nearing the close of a brilliant career.

When Mantle first came to the big leagues, it would have been difficult to imagine that he could someday inspire this sort of regard. Unlike Stan Musial and Willie Mays, he was not popular with the fans at first. Mickey had to earn their respect. And he did it against obstacles that few other great players have had to face.

Mickey was brought up to be a professional ballplayer. His father, Elven "Mutt" Mantle, was a miner who had always wanted to play ball himself. Although he was a fairly good semi-pro player, he never proved to be good enough to make the big leagues. When Mickey was born in Oklahoma in 1931, Mutt Mantle decided that he would try to make a big league ballplayer out of his son.

To give him an extra push, Mutt named his son after his favorite ballplayer—Mickey Cochrane, who had been a great catcher with the Athletics and the Tigers. Then, as soon as the boy was old enough to grip a bat, Mutt taught him to bat both left-handed and right-handed. He reasoned that a switch hitter would have an advantage over the other boys.

Mickey grew up to be a powerful teenager, with broad shoulders and great running speed. In high school he became a football star. It was in one of those high school games that Mickey suffered a serious leg injury. Afterward the doctors told him that he had osteomyelitis. This is a bone infection that is incurable, and it was to give Mickey a great deal of trouble in later years. He would never have "sound" legs.

But the youngster went right on playing his favorite sports. During Mickey's last year in high school, a scout for the Yankees heard about him and went to see him play. The scout was impressed by this strong lad who could hit the ball over the fence from either side of the plate. He was also impressed by Mantle's running speed. He offered Mickey a $1,500 bonus to sign a contract, and Mutt Mantle's son became the property of the New York Yankees.

Mickey played at Independence in 1949, and was promoted to another farm team at Joplin in 1950. There he led the league in almost every-thing—from hitting home runs to committing errors. In those days he was a shortstop. Though he could pick up the ground balls all right, his arm was so strong that he frequently threw the ball over the first baseman's head.

"The Yankees finally changed me from a short-stop to an outfielder," Mantle explained. "Mostly to protect the fans behind first base, I guess."

When a big league team knows it has a young

star coming to spring training, it usually makes sure that the sports world hears the news. But no young player ever received the publicity that Mickey got before he reported to the Yankees' camp in the spring of 1951. Some of the newspapermen joked that Mantle could save a lot of time by forgetting all about playing for the Yankees and going right to baseball's Hall of Fame at Cooperstown instead.

Writers crowded into the Yankee camp from all over the country. Everybody was anxious to see this blond young man who reportedly could hit the ball farther than Babe Ruth and run faster than Ty Cobb. To everybody's surprise, Mickey proved to be as good in spring training as the publicity men had predicted. He hit tremendous home runs—from *either* side of the plate!

Casey Stengel, the Yankees' manager, was delighted by Mantle's skills. He believed he saw in Mickey the natural ability that could make him the greatest player in the history of baseball. Mickey, he knew, was very inexperienced. He would have to work hard to make the best of his talent. But Casey loved to talk about his star rookie.

One day that spring Mickey was called out on a close play at third base. A newspaperman asked Stengel if he believed the umpire had missed the play.

142

Manager Casey Stengel (right) with one of his greatest rookies, Mickey Mantle.

"I don't know whether he was out or not," Casey said, "but I can see why the umpire thought he was. That kid got from first to third so fast they must have thought he ran across the pitcher's mound."

Though Mantle would have benefited from another year of experience in the minor leagues, Casey did not want to let him out of his sight. He decided to keep him with the Yankees. A pre-season game had been scheduled between the Yan-

143

kees and the Brooklyn Dodgers at Ebbets Field in Brooklyn. As a Dodger, Stengel had played there almost 40 years earlier when he was a young outfielder. On the day of the game he took Mantle out to Ebbets Field early in the morning to teach him how to play the tricky concrete wall in right field.

"I got him out there," Stengel said, "and told him I knew all about the wall because I had played it myself. The kid looked at me like he was astonished. I guess he thought I was born 58 years old and right away became the manager of the Yankees."

Casey admired Mickey as much as if he were his own son. He never tired of talking about him to anyone who would listen. But, to his dismay, Mickey was having a hard time hitting big league pitching. True, he walloped a tremendous home run every once in a while. But mostly he went up to bat and struck out. In July, Casey knew he had to make a change. He sent Mickey to the Yankees' top farm team at Kansas City.

No one ever felt more sorry for himself than Mickey Mantle did when he arrived in Kansas City. The bright dreams of a few months before had been shattered. Somehow it seemed very unfair. Everybody had been telling him how wonderful he was—how he was going to become the greatest player of all time.

While he was feeling sorry for himself, Mickey's father came to Kansas City to see him.

"I'm just not good enough for the majors, Dad," Mickey said.

Apparently he expected sympathy from his father, but he did not get it.

"If you're going to be a quitter," Mutt Mantle told his son, "then I think it's time you quit baseball and came back with me to work in the mines."

Mutt Mantle knew just the sort of words that would do his son some good. Mickey began to wallop the ball at Kansas City, and within a month he was back with the Yankees, helping them to win a pennant.

The 1951 World Series was an exciting one. The Yankees played the Giants. As a result, the two most highly rated rookies of their time were pitted against one another—Mickey Mantle and Willie Mays.

Again bad luck struck Mickey. Chasing a fly ball, he stepped into a drain pipe that someone had accidentally left open in the outfield grass.

"Mickey went down like he was shot," said Joe DiMaggio, who was playing beside him in the outfield that day.

The young player had suffered another serious leg injury. That winter he underwent an operation. In the spring of 1952 he was well enough to play center field for the Yankees, replacing

DiMaggio, who had retired. Mickey was still in a difficult position—he not only had to live up to all the publicity, but he also had to take the place of one of the finest players who ever wore a Yankees' uniform.

For a while Stengel was disappointed in his broad-backed young star. He patiently tried to correct Mickey's mistakes without much success.

"You tell him something," Stengel grumbled, "and he acts like you tell him nothing."

If Casey told him to rest his injured leg, Mickey would go out and hurt it again by playing basketball in his spare time. If he told him to stop trying to "kill" the ball, Mickey went up to bat and swung harder than ever. Then, when he struck out, he became very angry with himself.

The doctor places an ice pack on Mantle's right knee, injured during the 1951 Series.

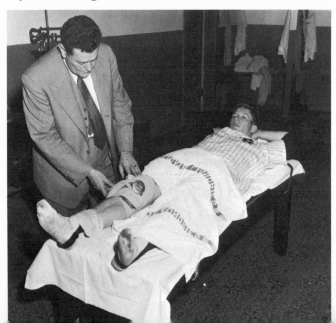

After he had struck out one day, Mickey came back to the dugout and angrily kicked the water cooler. Casey looked at him sadly.

"That water cooler ain't striking you out, son," he said.

Mickey did not seem to want to grow up. He and his roommate, Billy Martin, spent all of their time kidding around. One of their favorite pastimes, in the privacy of their hotel room, was to walk slowly toward each other, then whip out imaginary six-shooters and begin blasting away. "Bang-bang!" they would shout, just as they had seen it done in the Westerns. Then they would argue about who was the fastest on the draw.

Yet Mickey's talents were so great that he could not help being an outstanding player. His power at the plate was incredible. Not even the Babe had hit such long home runs. It was Mantle's homers that the newspapermen first described as "tape-measure jobs." He hit them so far that the writers and publicity men used to take tape measures and mark off the distance from home plate at which the ball landed.

Mantle led the league in 1955 with 37 home runs, then had one of his finest years in 1956 when he won the "triple crown." He led the league in homers (52), runs batted in (130) and batting (.353). After the season he was voted the Most Valuable Player in the American League.

Mickey connects for his 53rd homer of the 1961 season.

There is no doubt that Mantle was responsible in great part for the Yankees' success throughout most of his career. They won 12 pennants in Mickey's first 14 seasons. Yet leg injuries and other ailments often kept him from enjoying the spectacular seasons that the other leading stars have put together. Four times he was not able to be of much help to the Yankees in the World Series, and generally the team lost.

If injuries have prevented Mantle from setting

the records that otherwise might have been his, they have helped him in another way. His great courage in the face of misfortune caused both his teammates and the fans to respect him.

"Sometimes you feel tired and low," Joe Pepitone, a Yankee player, has said. "Then you think about Mickey and what he must be going through with the pain and you say to yourself, 'If he can do it the way he feels and the way he must be hurting, then I can do it too.'"

As he has grown older, Mickey has grown more mature too. In recent years his teammates have looked to him for leadership, just as other Yankee teams once looked to Joe DiMaggio. By his desire to win and by his courage in the face of pain, he has swung the fans to his side.

And that is why the fans in Detroit rose to their feet on that afternoon in 1968 and cheered this aging player. Many must have felt, like Denny McLain, that Mickey Mantle was their idol.

HENRY AARON

"When I go up to the plate I've got a bat in my hands, and all the pitcher has got is a ball," Henry Aaron once said. "I figure that makes it all in my favor."

The records make it clear that Henry has figured the situation correctly. This slender, lazy-looking fellow has used his sharp eyes and marvelous wrists to pull himself into the highest ranks among baseball's power hitters. He hits the ball to all fields, and he beats out bunts as expertly as he slams long home runs. At one time or another he has led the National League in just about every hitting department.

Yet Aaron seldom is able to recall what his own records are at the moment. Asked by a reporter one day what his batting average was, Henry simply shrugged.

"Anybody with a pencil can figure batting averages," he said. "So you do the figuring and I'll do the hitting."

Henry Aaron is one of those "natural" hitters who sometimes prove to be more successful than boys who are taught the right way to do things from the very beginning. He was a professional ballplayer before he learned that he was holding the bat completely wrong. He had never noticed the "right" way to pick up a bat. Henry, a right-handed hitter, held it cross-handed, placing his left hand above his right. Horrified, the manager of Henry's first professional team ordered him to shift his hands around. Even so, for a long time Henry continued to bat cross-handed when he thought the manager was not watching him very closely.

When he came to the major leagues, Henry didn't realize that a ballplayer does not hold his bat with the label turned toward the pitcher. One of his teammates on the Braves noticed how he held his bat, and shouted:

"Hey, Henry, watch the label."

"I get paid for hitting," Henry called back, "not for reading."

Henry Aaron was born in Alabama in 1934. His father, a laborer, had eight children to support.

"But we owned our own home," Henry says with pride. "We helped our father build it. We didn't have any new lumber, but we found lumber that they took out of old houses that were torn down. I'd kick the nails out of the old boards. The house wasn't bad, and we owned it ourselves."

Henry played high school football in Mobile, but he liked baseball best. After his graduation, he signed a contract to play with the Indianapolis Clowns of the Negro American League. He was an infielder in those days. Someone told the Braves that the Clowns had a good-looking young player, and a couple of the team's officials went to Buffalo to watch Henry play.

"It rained like crazy that day," one of the Braves' officials said, "and we didn't get much of a look at Aaron. We saw him hit a couple of times, though. We didn't know if he could field or not, but we liked the way he swung the bat."

The Braves bought Aaron's contract from the Clowns and sent him to their minor league team at Eau Claire, Wisconsin. Henry batted .336 there in 1952. The next year he was promoted to Jacksonville. There he quickly became the most dangerous hitter in the league. But, like every other ballplayer, Aaron occasionally fell into a slump. After suffering through several hitless days, Henry finally began hitting the ball again.

"How come you snapped out of your slump?"

Hank Aaron, 19-year-old second baseman for the Jacksonville Braves.

Jim Andrews, one of his teammates, asked him.

"Oh, I just picked up the phone and called Mr. Stan Musial and he told me what to do," Henry said, without cracking a smile.

Andrews repeated the story to the other players. A week or so later a sports writer asked Henry if he had had any more conversations with Musial.

"What are you talking about?" Aaron wanted to know.

"Didn't you tell Jim Andrews that you'd called Musial and he'd told you how to get out of the slump?" the sports writer asked.

Aaron's face broke into a big grin. "Oh, that! Why I'm liable to tell Jim Andrews *anything.*"

Henry had a fine season at Jacksonville, leading the league in batting and runs batted in. The Braves told him to report to their training camp in Florida in the spring of 1954.

No one expected Aaron to play with the Braves that year. Despite his fine records in the minors, he was only 20 years old and he was not a very skilled infielder. Then several of the Braves' outfielders were injured. The Milwaukee manager —the Braves played in Milwaukee in those days— gave Henry a chance in the outfield. Not only did Henry hit big league pitching all through spring training but he proved himself to be a good outfielder as well. When the Braves came north to open the season, Henry Aaron was in the starting line-up.

For a while the National League pitchers thought that this inexperienced young hitter would be easy to fool. They threw bad pitches to Henry, trying to make him "fish" for the ball. Henry went after them all right, but soon the pitchers learned that he could hit the bad pitches as well as the good ones.

"Aaron's strike zone is from the top of his head right down to his toes," one manager said.

During a close game with the Dodgers, Don Newcombe did not want to feed Aaron a fat pitch.

He threw the ball down around his ankles, but Henry golfed it off the left-field wall for a double.

Newcombe was furious. "The next time I'll throw one *under* the plate," he shouted to Aaron. "Then let's see you hit that!"

Henry batted .280 as a rookie in 1954, and .314 the next season. By this time he had gained great confidence in his own ability. In the spring of 1956 he predicted to a sports writer that he would lead the National League in batting that season. He did—finishing with an average of .328.

But not even Henry predicted all the good things that were in store for him in 1957. The Braves had a fine team that year, and Aaron was their star. He suddenly blossomed into a power hitter. Home runs boomed off his bat, and enemy pitchers got the shakes when he stepped into the batter's box.

The Braves grabbed the league lead and headed for the pennant. Nearing the season's end, they needed only one more victory to clinch the flag. On September 23 they played the Cardinals at Milwaukee. The Cardinals did not give up without a fight and carried the game into extra innings. The score was tied, 2–2, in the last half of the 11th inning when Aaron came to bat against the Cardinals' veteran pitcher, Billy Muffett.

No one had hit a home run against Muffett all season. But Aaron, timing the pitch perfectly,

The jubilant Braves carry slugger Hank Aaron off the field after his two-run homer produced a 4–2 win over the Cardinals, clinching the pennant.

slashed at one of Muffett's curve balls and drove it over the left-field fence for a home run. The crowd surged out of the stands as the pennant-winning Braves carried Aaron off the field on their shoulders. That night Milwaukee was the scene of one of the wildest and happiest celebrations ever seen in an American city.

The records proved how valuable Aaron had

157

been to the Braves in their struggle to win the pennant. His batting average that season was .322. But, more important, he hit with great power, leading the league with his 44 home runs and his 132 runs batted in. He was voted the Most Valuable Player in the National League. And Henry went right on slugging in the World Series. He hit three homers and batted .393 as the Braves beat the Yankees.

Pitchers, of course, expect a big strong fellow like Babe Ruth or Hank Greenberg or Mickey Mantle to be able to break up a ball game with one powerful swing of his bat. But Aaron has never satisfied their image of a slugger—until the ball has disappeared over a distant wall. He has neither broad shoulders nor bulging muscles. Nor does he look especially mean as he stands at the plate. In fact, many pitchers think he looks sleepy.

"Aaron's the only hitter I ever saw who seems like he goes to sleep between pitches," commented Robin Roberts, the great right-handed pitcher of the Philadelphia Phillies.

Henry wastes no movements, on the field or off. He seems to chase fly balls in long, lazy strides. But he always catches up with them. And when he *has* to run, there are few men in baseball who are able to keep up with him. "I think Henry could steal 100 bases a year if the need came up," one of his teammates says. And the manager of

*Outfielder Aaron falls to his knees as he goes after
a Yankee hit in the 1967 Series.*

an opposing team in the National League says: "If you think Aaron isn't fast, just try to make a double play on any ball he hits."

Henry, of course, likes to give the impression that he is a slow-moving—and slow-thinking—ballplayer. In that way he sometimes catches the other team with its guard down. He has found that it is smart to pretend that you are dumb.

"Would you rather play the outfield or the infield," a newspaperman once asked Henry.

"Oh, I like the outfield," he said.

"Why?"

"Out there I don't have as much to do, especially not as much thinking."

It is quite true that Henry Aaron likes to sleep. When the Braves are not playing, Henry is likely to be stretched out somewhere, engaged in some serious sleeping.

"Man, I'm just making up for all the sleep I lost when I played with the Indianapolis Clowns," Henry says. "We traveled by bus. It seems like I spent most of my time sitting up on a bus going from one town to another. We never stopped traveling—as soon as a game was over, on to the next town."

But no player on the field is more wide-awake than Aaron once the ball game begins. He watches every move that the other team makes. He seems to possess an extra sense that lets him know what the pitcher is going to throw, and he adjusts his swing accordingly.

"Do you expect the pitcher to throw you a certain type of pitch in a certain situation?" a reporter asked Aaron.

"Sometimes I look for the curve ball," Henry answered, "and sometimes I look for the fast ball. But when that count goes to three-and-two I just look for the *baseball*."

Like a smart quarterback on the football field, Aaron always has his eye on the way the opposing team positions itself. He realizes that sometimes a single is as important as a home run. If he catches the third baseman playing far back on the infield for him, Henry likes to lay down a bunt and beat it out.

"It helps me next time up, too," he says. "Maybe the third baseman will come in a little too far then, looking for me to bunt, and I can slash the ball past him."

Aaron sometimes upsets people because he is not very talkative. A sports writer who tries to interview him may find that Henry simply answers his questions with a "yes" or a "no." He is not being rude. He just likes to conserve his energy, whether he is on the playing field or in front of a flock of reporters. It is hard for him to pay attention very long to social graces. Besides, he has a hard time remembering people's names.

"Who are the pitchers that give you the most trouble?" a reporter asked Aaron during his early days in the National League.

"Well, that Robin Roberts is pretty tough," Henry answered. "But I don't know the names of any other pitchers."

Pitchers on other teams need not feel insulted. One reporter, who wanted to talk to Henry's roommate, learned that Henry did not even know his friend's name.

"Who is your roommate?" the reporter asked him.

"Felix," Henry replied.

"Felix who?" the reporter asked.

Aaron was silent for a moment. "Felix . . . Oh, you know—he's our shortstop."

The reporter finally figured out that Henry was talking about Felix Mantilla.

On another occasion Aaron was fined $25 by Ford Frick, who was then the Commissioner of Baseball. It seems that he had been playing ball in Florida early in the spring before the training camps had officially opened.

"Do you know that you've been fined by Ford Frick?" one of the Braves' officials asked him.

"Ford Frick?" Aaron said, wrinkling his brow into a frown. "Who's he?"

Meanwhile, Henry always remembers to swing his bat when a pitch comes anywhere near the

Number 44 takes a powerful swing at the ball.

plate. He led the league in hitting again in 1959, this time with a sizzling .355 average. He has led the league in hitting home runs three times since 1957. Henry moved to Atlanta with the rest of the Braves. But he continued to run the bases and roam the outfield just as fast as he had to—which was still about as fast as almost any other player in the game. Many experts believe that Henry, by the time he retires from baseball, will have built up a lifetime home-run total second only to Babe Ruth's.

Sports writer Jim Murray once pointed out that Henry's last name begins with *two* "a's." "Henry Aaron," Murray said, "leads the league both alphabetically and athletically."

And that's no joke!

INDEX

ABOUT THE AUTHOR

Frank Graham, Jr. has been involved in baseball for most of his life. The son of a well-known sports writer, he was the publicity director of the old Brooklyn Dodgers, an editor with *Sport* Magazine, and is a regular contributor to *Sports Illustrated*. He is also the author of two other Major League Library books, *Great Pennant Races of the Major Leagues* and *Great No-Hit Games of the Major Leagues*. He lives in Milbridge, Maine.